NO SUCH THING
AS A BAD DAY

"Titles come and go, and White House chiefs of staff can exit faster than they entered. But Jordan, at fifty-five, would have you believe he has larger fish to fry than congressmen and Cabinet secretaries wanting fifteen minutes with the president of the United States, not to mention the door-pounding Washington media. . . . The architect of Jimmy Carter's improbable nomination for the presidency tells how quickly power and position fade to irrelevance and how one's sense of proportion can change."

—*The Atlanta Journal-Constitution*

"Jordan serves up wise counsel, instructive insights, and important hope to the millions of American families afflicted with this dreaded disease. Along the way, he offers delicious, sometimes biting, political perspectives."

—*The Wall Street Journal*

"Sound, upbeat advice . . . [Jordan] offers cancer sufferers and their families ways to combat the disease by . . . being positive and proactive."

—*Library Journal*

"An inspiring journey of a man who feels lucky to be alive . . . a story worth hearing and a story worth reading."

—*The Huntsville Times* (AL)

NO SUCH THING AS A BAD DAY

A MEMOIR BY

HAMILTON JORDAN

FOREWORD BY JIMMY CARTER

POCKET BOOKS

New York London Toronto Sydney Singapore

POCKET BOOKS, a division of Simon & Schuster, Inc.
1230 Avenue of the Americas, New York, NY 10020

ISBN: 0-7434-1920-0

First Pocket Books trade paperback printing May 2001

10 9 8 7 6 5 4 3 2 1

POCKET and colophon are registered trademarks of Simon & Schuster, Inc.

Cover design by Brigid Pearson,
front cover photo by David Hathcox

Printed in the U.S.A.

FOREWORD

The fascinating journey detailed in these pages will arouse the interest of every reader.

Imagine an author who has survived attacks from three different kinds of cancer, and is able to describe these experiences with courage and good humor.

Imagine that this same young man — a quarter of a century ago at the age of twenty-seven — analyzed one of the most complicated and daunting political challenges in American history, and planned the basic strategy for a campaign that brought an unknown Georgia governor into the White House.

As a young Southerner, Hamilton Jordan's personal tribulations while serving as White House chief-of-staff are the stuff of which fiction is ordinarily made. These challenges took on a bizarre and damaging life of their own when Hamilton was faced with a barrage of false accusations from men who lied in order to reduce their own prison sentences.

As a boy, Hamilton saw his Uncle Clarence Jordan become the founder of a racially integrated farm in deep South Georgia in the 1940s. He witnessed the intense hatred that this aroused among the Ku Klux Klansmen, whose bombs, fires, and bullets did not deter Clarence Jordan from demonstrating his Christian faith in action.

Fifteen years later, Hamilton was on the scene when Martin Luther King Jr. began his early civil rights marches in Albany, Georgia.

During the Vietnam conflict, the author volunteered to serve, but, when he was physically disqualified for combat, went there on a humanitarian mission. Instead of the Viet Cong, his unsuspected adversary turned out to be Agent Orange, an almost fatal encounter he later described to Admiral Elmo Zumwalt, whose order to use the chemical herbicide resulted in the death of his own son.

In summary, this is an astonishing collection of adventures and observations, woven into a dramatic account that helps to clarify some of the mysteries of our nation's recent history. But above all, Hamilton Jordan's book provides reassurance for cancer patients and members of every family who face the challenge of this disease.

Hamilton's story offers a rare combination of insight, wry humor, and real inspiration.

JIMMY CARTER
Plains, Georgia

DEDICATION

This book is dedicated with love and admiration

to *Kathleen Jordan*

*— my eleven-year-old daughter — whose courage, joy, and spirit
in dealing with a chronic disease inspires me and all who are
fortunate to know her.*

*Her mother, her two brothers — Hamilton Jr. and Alexander —
and I are very proud of her and grateful to her for her example.*

Table of Contents

PART ONE

PART TWO

PART ONE

FIRST TIME AROUND

I remember it like it was yesterday.

I was lying in my hospital bed. My doctor had just left to review the tissue report with the pathologist . . . he promised to come back within the hour. I had been in the hospital now for five days and had had every test in the book. And it all came down to a person sitting in a laboratory somewhere peering into a microscope at my cells and deciding what kind of cancer I had . . . and whether I would live or die. Would it be curable, or even treatable? Would I have a fighting chance, or be left to hope for a miracle, racing around the world to off-beat clinics searching for a cure?

My dear mother and sister made small talk to pass time. A nurse's aide brought in a form for me to fill out evaluating the hospital services.

"Have you enjoyed your stay, Mr. Jordan?" she asked.

"I'll tell you in an hour," I joked. She didn't understand.

I found myself knotting up the bed sheet in my hand. The emotional mask that I had been wearing for my family's sake was close to being shattered. Just to escape, I turned on the television and surfed from channel to channel, hoping to be distracted, and was startled to see a picture of myself on the local CBS affiliate. I turned the volume up in time to hear, "CBS has learned that former Carter aide Hamilton Jordan is in an Atlanta hospital and has been diagnosed with inoperable lung cancer."

Panic gripped my body as I looked at an old photo of myself on the television screen and these strange words sunk in.

My mother's face dropped and my sister watched me closely for a reaction. Then logic returned. If my doctor, who just left my room, didn't know what I had, how in the hell did CBS News know? Like so many other times, the media had only half the story right.

The panic caused by the news report subsided as we continued to wait. Suddenly, my room was flooded with doctors: the oncologists, my pulmonary specialist, the radiologist. I tried to read them like a jury . . . one was smiling slightly, the others were not. What did it all mean?

The radiologist broke the ice. "Hamilton, when more than one doctor comes into your room, it is usually pretty good news."

"All I ever wanted was a fighting chance."

"Well, Mr. Jordan," my lead doctor said, "you certainly have that." He paused, glanced down at a written report and looked up. "You have diffuse histiocytic lymphoma. Ten years ago, this would have been a death sentence, but this is an area where we have made progress . . . there are a number of treatments that are reasonably effective in dealing with this disease."

I stuck on one word. "Reasonably, doctor? What does that mean?"

"This is one of those 'good news, bad news' situations. The bad news is that you have a very aggressive cancer. The good news is that aggressive cancers divide rapidly, which means that they are particularly vulnerable to chemotherapy and radiation at the time of cell division. We've got to find a treatment your cancer will respond to."

He went on to tell me that I would need to undergo further tests, but that the evidence at this point was that the cancer was confined to my chest area. "We plan to radiate your chest. The bottom line is that we have a good shot at curing this."

That was too vague, and I learned for the first of many times that cancer patients should only ask questions if they are prepared to hear the answer. "What is a 'good shot,' doctor?"

"Well, every patient is different. . . ."

"Just quantify it for me!" I interrupted.

"I don't like to use numbers, Mr. Jordan, but if you insist. . . ."

"I do," I said firmly.

"About half of the patients who have non-Hodgkins lymphoma would achieve a remission with the therapy we will give you. Half of those will be free of disease five years out."

I was doing the math in my head. "So overall, I have about a 25 percent chance of being in the group that obtains a remission AND is cancer-free five years later?"

"That's about right, Mr. Jordan."

I was devastated to hear my chances of being alive reduced to statistics, but I had asked for it. And from that point on, I insisted that doctors avoid vague terms and quantify my situation. When the stats were favorable, I believed them and clung to them. When they were discouraging, I either tossed them aside or made up my mind to be one of those who beat the odds.

But when the doctors left my room that afternoon, I was faced with the cold, harsh fact that the odds greatly favored the cancer winning this battle, not me.

I didn't sleep much that night.

The story had actually begun on August 24, 1985, a day frozen forever in my memory.

I knew something was wrong when my family doctor sent me to the hospital for my annual chest X ray, which he had routinely taken in his office for fifteen years. A couple of hours later as we sat in his office, he talked quietly on the phone to the radiologist. I strained to hear, but all I could make out was, "I understand, yes . . . I understand."

He hung up the phone, turned away as if to avoid contact, slid the X rays out of the large brown envelope, turned them upright one by one and lined them up on the illuminated viewer. What had taken him seconds seemed like hours. He took a deep breath, pointed with his finger to a smoky area on one film and said slowly, "Hamilton, I hate to tell you this, but you have an abnormal chest film."

He paused to watch me as his words sank in. "This spot here is some kind of mass . . . some kind of growth."

"Could it be a cancerous growth?" I asked quietly.

"Yes," he said slowly, picking his words carefully, "and most likely it is a cancerous growth, but we will not know for sure until we take a biopsy."

I was stunned and just sat there, staring at the film. I felt like someone had suddenly pulled a plug and all the energy and feeling were flowing from my body. I had a surreal sense of standing apart from this bizarre scene and watching myself sitting in the examination room, talking with my doctor friend, asking the predictable questions:

"Do we know for sure it is cancer?"

"What kind of cancers would grow in that area?"

"What can I do?"

"Will I live?"

After he had repeated six or eight times, "We won't know any more until we do the biopsy," I stopped asking questions and was ready to go home.

My doctor kindly offered to drive me home so that he could tell Dorothy, my wife. I thanked him but said that I wanted to be alone.

I was barely out of the parking lot when Dorothy called on the car phone to report something cute our eighteen-month-old son, Hamilton Jr., had said. Later, she would tell me that she had sensed something different in my voice. "What's wrong?" she asked.

This was not the way to tell her, I thought. I needed to be able to hold her in my arms, comfort her and be comforted, but I couldn't hold back. I needed her to know and simply blurted it out: "Richard found a mass in my chest and thinks it's cancer!"

Dorothy was shattered. She tried to be strong and brave for me, but I could feel the fear oozing out of her every pore. For the first of many times, I realized that it is often more difficult to be the loved one than the cancer patient.

I will never forget taking Hamilton Jr. for a walk in his stroller that same afternoon. I welcomed getting away from the house and from Dorothy and having time to think . . . but I could only think about him. I stopped, picked him up, and hugged him as I cried softly so as to not scare him. Would I live to see his second birthday? Or his third? I fought back tears every time I looked at him and was thankful he did not understand that something bad was going on with his "da-da."

Dorothy and I spent the evening on the phone alerting family and friends . . . these were terrible calls to make.

Everyone tried to be optimistic and struggled to say the right thing.

"Maybe it is just a virus you caught in Vietnam," offered my mother, who was battling lung cancer herself.

"It could be benign," my sister suggested.

"You hear about mistaken X rays all the time," a close friend said.

While my family was filled with wishful thinking, I chose to look at it differently. This was definitely serious, probably cancerous, and the big question was whether or not it was curable. I started off thinking that my chances were not very good while my family was hoping and praying for tropical diseases and mistaken readings of my film.

I checked into the hospital the next morning for a complete battery of tests. It would take a couple of days. I resolved to be brave for my family. If I fell apart, I would be no good for myself or for them. I hid my very real fears and spent the next several days cracking jokes and trying to make the best of a miserable situation.

While I was waiting for the report from the biopsy, a friend who happened to be a professional counselor stuck her head through the door. "In the mood for some company?"

"You bet . . . am I glad to see you," I replied.

She sat down on the side of the bed, grasped my hand, and — fighting back tears — said, "I have been thinking about you and praying for you."

My first thought was that she was going to have to pull herself together before she could help me. "I appreciate your prayers but right now I would gladly trade them for some advice on how to get my head straight. We've been on a roller coaster, and I have to settle down and live with this thing, whatever it is."

"Hamilton, the best thing you can do is to understand the various stages people go through when confronting a serious illness."

I nodded. That made sense.

She continued: "Most people deny their illness initially. They hope that they will wake up the next morning from a bad dream. They refuse to face reality by denying reality.

"The second stage is usually anger," she continued. "People get mad at the world, at their family members, themselves and at God. They ask, 'Why me? What have I done to deserve this?'

"Next, people usually bargain with God by making a promise that they will do something worthwhile with their lives if they are allowed to live."

"Finally, patients become depressed, but out of that feeling of despair, people ultimately face their reality. This is acceptance — when a person puts aside his anger and denial, looks squarely at his problem, accepts and deals with it."

"Look," I said, "I'm not trying to be different and maybe I am just hiding my real feelings, but what you describe is not the way I feel. Denial? Deny what? I've got a mass in my chest the size of an apple. I have seen it on the X ray, know it's there . . . so there's no use in denying it. Angry? At whom? I have lived a great life and have been blessed with much more than I deserve. I don't want to die, but if I died tomorrow, I wouldn't have much room to complain. I don't know 'Why me?' but 'Why not me?' Maybe God gave me this disease because he thinks that I am strong enough to handle it."

"Bargaining with God?" I continued. "The God that I believe in has all the cards. . . . I don't think that God has to sit down and negotiate with His creations. What am I supposed to do, say that I will be a television evangelist if I am cured?"

She smiled.

"I don't know if I want to be cured that badly," I added with a grin.

"Hamilton, you have totally blown my theory and obviously you have already accepted the reality of your disease."

"Is that okay?" I asked.

"It is terrific!" she said as she bent over and gave me a big hug. "It's terrific!"

———————

LEARNING ABOUT CANCER . . . THE HARD WAY

Unfortunately, I know a hell of a lot about cancer.

Back in 1975, on a beach vacation with my parents, my father had complained of sharp pain in his hip, which he dismissed as "arthritis." Weeks later, my mother called to report that my father had been hospitalized with something she would only describe on the phone as "serious." I rushed home and went directly to the doctor's office. He held my father's bone scan against a light, revealing a perfect outline of his skeleton with what looked like twenty or thirty spots sprinkled across his frame. His body looked like a Christmas tree strung with white lights.

"Those are 'hot spots,'" the doctor explained. "Each of them is a cancerous growth in the bone. I'm sorry to have to tell you this, but your dad has metastatic prostate cancer."

I bombarded him with questions. . . . How did this happen? What was his prognosis? Was it curable? Would my father die?

"Sometimes we find a lump in a man's prostate gland during a physical. We do a biopsy. If it's cancer and there's no evidence of spread, we take the prostate out. If we are lucky, that's the end of it. The poor patient is impotent and incontinent as a result of the surgery, but he has a chance for a full life. Often, by the time we feel the lump in the prostate the horse is already out of the barn in many patients; the cancer has spread, and — like with your dad — it is already in the bones. Once the cancer escapes the prostate, it is incurable."

Soon afterwards, my father began his treatment, had his testicles removed and began taking female hormones, a course of treatment that usually puts prostate cancer into remission for a period of time. His was a textbook case as he enjoyed two years of quality living, learning even to joke about the enlarged breasts that resulted from the female hormones. Then, as they almost always do, the hormones lost their effect and the cancer came roaring back in his bones. He died within the year.

CAMP SUNSHINE

But it was at Camp Sunshine that I really learned about cancer and the enduring lessons of life.

Shortly after we married and several years before my first bout with cancer, Dorothy — a pediatric oncology nurse — organized Camp Sunshine, one of the first non-profit camps in the country for children with cancer. New to Atlanta, Dorothy was a dynamo: raising money; recruiting campers from reluctant parents not inclined to give up their sick children for even a week; recruiting volunteer counselors; organizing a sophisticated medical clinic fully staffed by pediatric oncologists and nurses from Emory; and organizing an outstanding camp program for these special children.

It was a major undertaking. Early on, I tried to help a little too much, second guessing some decisions she had made. Dorothy told me in no uncertain terms to back off, that this was not a political campaign but her project. I did, and ever since, Camp Sunshine has been Dorothy's volunteer project with my playing a minor, supportive role. (I am the perennial MC for Talent Night . . . one year I was M.C. Hammer-ton and another time, Judge Ito.)

We started with only thirty-eight campers and twenty-five volunteers. Today, Camp Sunshine has a year-round program for over four hundred children and their families: two weeks of summer camp, a family weekend that addresses the problems that affect the siblings and parents, a ski trip to Colorado for amputees and the physically challenged, a trip to Washington for our teenagers, an "Outward Bound" program and many other activities. Camp Sunshine has had a major impact on our lives, especially by giving us the opportunity to witness time and time again dramatic demonstrations of the power of the mind and attitude to alter the course of disease.

My favorite memory is of Corey Grier, a good-looking black teenager. A natural leader with a ready wit and generous spirit, Corey drew boys and girls of all ages to him like a magnet. He also had a tough cancer in his colon and battled it with great courage for several years. Finally, the tumor got the upper hand.

In July 1985, the doctors told Corey he had a short time to live. Corey calmly told his doctors that he

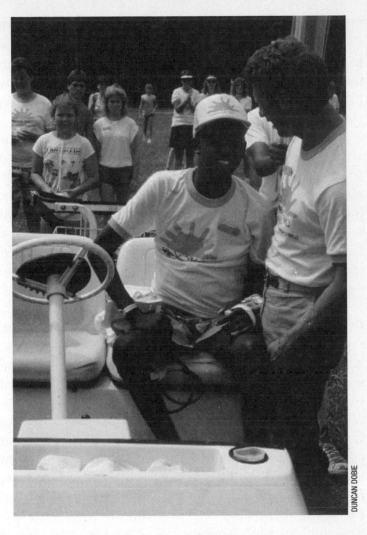

COREY GRIER DAY AT CAMP SUNSHINE

intended to live until June (1986) so he could return to Camp Sunshine to tell his friends goodbye and celebrate his seventeenth birthday that same week. The doctors humored Corey, but told his parents that he would be lucky to make it to Christmas and would never live to the next summer.

Eleven months later, a gaunt but smiling Corey was airlifted to Camp Sunshine on a helicopter to celebrate "Corey Grier Day." The campers held up hand-made signs, clapped and yelled excitedly as the helicopter touched down on the football field. Everyone crowded around Corey, reaching out to touch him or to slap a "high five." Several older campers lifted him carefully from the chopper and carried him gently to a specially decorated golf cart.

Surrounded on all sides by counselors and campers, Corey looked like the Pied Piper as he led the crowd to the lodge where we celebrated with ice cream, cake, and stories. Corey stayed for only a few hours but had a great time. As he rode back to the athletic field, he was talking a mile a minute, emotionally exhilarated from his visit. He even told one camper that he might live until the next Camp Sunshine. As Corey was hoisted into the helicopter, the harsh reality of the moment sunk in. The chopper paused about twenty feet from the ground and did a "360" so that we could all see Corey's smiling face one last time before he disappeared in the blue summer sky. We waved and waved, hoping that our forced smiles hid our tears. By the time the chopper was out of sight, several hundred people were wiping their eyes and hugging one another.

Corey returned to Egleston Hospital that night, celebrated his seventeenth birthday the next morning with his family and some favorite nurses, and died peacefully that afternoon.

Corey's story is just one of many of the brave children who have touched our lives in indescribable ways. They have taught us how to live and sometimes have shown us how to die.

DECISION TIME

With my biopsy behind me and my diagnosis complete, it was time to begin treatment. But what was the best treatment? My doctors told me that they could treat me locally. But was there a doctor out there somewhere who was having remarkable success curing people with my type of lymphoma?

In what I would later come to believe was one of many small miracles in my life, a doctor friend flew in from out of town just to be with me. I was counting on him to calm me down, to tell me everything was going to be okay.

Instead, he shook me up. He put his hand on my shoulder, and simply said, "Old friend, you have got to take charge of your own medical care."

"What?" I said. "Here I am worrying about dying. Don't I have enough to think about with my young wife and baby . . . and you wander in here and tell me I have got to be responsible for the medical decisions?"

"That is exactly right!" he shot back. "Tell me who has a greater stake in the decisions that have to be made than you do?"

The minute he said it, I knew he was right, and from that moment on, I did take charge. The stakes were too high. . . . I could not afford to be passive. I had to have the peace of mind of knowing that whatever treatment I received was the best available.

I shared my candid feelings with my own doctor that afternoon. He agreed to help me explore all my options. That night, I gave an orderly twenty-five dollars to sneak me out of the hospital and wheel me over to the library. In a few hours, I knew a hell of a lot about diffuse histiocytic lymphoma. While there was much I did not comprehend, I was able to understand the broad challenges that faced me.

This kind of lymphoma was usually aggressive, was considered incurable until recently and had almost always spread to different sites in the body when it was diagnosed — hence the name "diffuse." It was obvious from recent journal articles and clinical trials currently taking place that there were several centers in the United States that specialized in treating lymphomas.

In every article I read, "staging" the disease was

critically important. A test known as the "lymph-angiagram" was essential to assess the spread of lymphoma and could even detect internal changes in an individual node that might indicate lymphoma. This old-fashioned, painstaking test required that a skilled technician find tiny lymph veins in each toe and "push" dye into the veins which would then show up on a scan.

When I asked my doctor about the lymphangiagram, he called it "outdated" and declared that it had been replaced by the CAT scan. "We don't have anyone here who could even do a lymphangiagram anymore," he explained.

The moment that he said that, I made a resolute decision to go somewhere else for my treatment. Within twenty-four hours, I had talked with five cancer centers around the world that were developing experimental treatments for non-Hodgkin's lymphoma. The name of the National Cancer Institute in Bethesda, Maryland, popped up time and again for their pioneering work on lymphomas. In my research, I would ask the doctor or nurse whom I was talking to, "What would you do if you had my disease?" A majority said that they would to go NCI . . . others mentioned NCI as one of several options.

I made contact with a doctor at NCI who told me that they were getting 60 to 70 percent of their non-Hodgkin's lymphoma into complete remission and that 70 percent of those in remission were cancer-free after several years. I did some quick math in my head. "That means that you have a 50 percent cure rate?"

"That's right, and if your disease is localized and early, your odds could be slightly better."

I asked about having the NCI experimental treatment given to me in Atlanta so I would not have to move my family.

"Look, Mr. Jordan, you usually have one shot at curing lymphoma. I would want to have my treatment administered at the place where it had been developed, especially when that place has the broadest possible experience in treating lymphomas. Why go for a reproduction when you can have the original?"

It was difficult to leave our Atlanta doctors and the community where we have so many personal and emotional ties. And it was a logistical nightmare to contemplate uprooting our little boy and leaving the comforts of home. But this was my life, and I had to take my very best shot. There is a lot of difference between a 25 percent chance of cure (which I had been offered locally) and 50 percent when you are dealing with your life.

"I'll be there tomorrow," I said.

While packing, I got a call from NCI with an offer to have a limousine pick me up at the airport. I told the well-meaning staffer that I appreciated the gesture, but that I didn't want or expect VIP treatment. "Spread the word up there, please, that I want to be treated like Joe Smith."

There were selfish reasons for my attitude. During the Iranian hostage crisis, I had to negotiate with the Shah of

Iran and his medical team on the logistics of his treatment for cancer (ironically lymphoma) and had seen first-hand how doctors tend to overreact to public figures. In some instances, the doctors become too conservative and are not willing to take the normal risks required in dealing with a serious medical problem. On the other extreme, some tend to "overtreat" public figures, become too aggressive and take too many risks. I didn't want either extreme — I simply wanted the best care that NCI would give an ordinary patient.

I had also seen the egos of doctors and patients result in less than ideal medical care. The Shah of Iran needed to have his spleen removed and insisted that Dr. Michael DeBakey, the great heart surgeon, perform the operation. Dr. DeBakey, who had not personally removed a spleen in years, took the Shah's spleen out. Later, the Shah died in Egypt of cancer and complications from the surgery.

Conversely, when President Reagan was shot, the White House doctor opted not to have "the best" doctors brought in but insisted that the doctors on duty in the emergency room who dealt with gunshot wounds every day treat the president. Some doctors credit that decision with saving the president's life.

Once I got to NCI, I was indeed treated like Joe Smith and put on an accelerated batch of tests.

"We are going to work your ass off, Mr. Jordan," one friendly young doctor teased. And they did. In two days, I had a spinal tap, a repeat bone marrow, constant blood work, a liver scan, a brain and bone scan, and a liver biopsy monitored by a scope that was inserted into my abdomen by an incision through my belly button.

And finally the lymphangiogram, the test they were unable to do in Atlanta that had motivated me to look around in the first place.

This is a delightful four-hour procedure where you have to lie perfectly still while they cut tiny holes in your toes to find a lymph vein through which they inject dye, which illuminates your entire lymphatic system on X ray. The lymphangiogram revealed one or two suspicious nodes below my diaphragm that were not enlarged but that looked "funny" in the words of the radiologist. If there was cancer in those nodes, it would totally change my "staging" (the extent of disease) and the treatment they would give me.

"We want to know the truth," my doctor said. "If there is cancer in your abdomen, we need to know so we can adjust our treatment accordingly. I want to stick a needle through your belly and sample these two nodes." He went on to explain that this was a slightly risky procedure as the nodes which he would biopsy were adjacent to a major artery.

"If you want to know, I want to know," I said quickly. In the short time I had been there, I had developed absolute confidence in the NCI medical staff.

After giving me a mild sedative and a local painkiller, the radiologist pulled out what he described as "my favorite Japanese needle," which was about two feet long.

I asked if I could watch.

"Only if you promise not to faint," he said as he moved the table around so I could clearly see the X ray monitor. He quickly stuck the needle in my abdomen.

"I promise not to faint if you promise not to stick that damn thing into my heart or artery."

He laughed and with sure, steady hands, probed and pushed until the tip of the needle was about a half-inch from the target node. "The challenge here," he explained, "is that this node is not firmly attached to anything. I have to spear it free-floating to get a good sample."

I wished he had not told me that, turned my head away from the monitor, and gulped a deep breath. Maybe I shouldn't feel so cocky. The thought had barely crossed my mind when I felt the needle move.

"Gotcha!" said the doctor.

I turned quickly to the monitor and saw the needle stuck in the node like a spear in a fish.

I breathed a sign of relief.

He quickly drew the sample tissue out of the needle, placed it in a vial, and held it up to the light.

"Mr. Jordan, I got a good piece of the bottom of this node, but I would like to get a piece of that other node if you'll let me. It is important to know what's going on in there."

Sounding more confident than I felt, I said, "Go ahead."

In another minute, he had penetrated the top of the

second node and drawn the long needle out of my belly.

I shook his hand and thanked him. "With an aim like that, you must hunt birds!"

He shook his head. "I am a terrible shot."

"I wish you hadn't told me that."

It turned out that the lymphangiagram saved my life. The needle biopsy found cancer in one of the nodes in my stomach. This important new fact completely changed my staging and their treatment.

Without the lymphangiagram, I would have been staged a "1-A," which meant that the doctors believed the cancer was confined to my chest and could have been treated with radiation. I would have had my chest radiated, the mass would have probably melted away and for some period of time (my doctors guessed several months), we would have believed we had killed the cancer. But the cancer in my abdomen would have been unaffected by the radiation to my chest, would have spread throughout my body and greatly reduced the possibility of my achieving a remission or a cure.

I considered the fact that it had spread to my abdomen a tremendous setback. "How bad is that?" I asked my doctor.

"Not bad at all . . . at least we know now where we stand. We will zap you with this new cocktail. And it has been working pretty good. You have early disease, localized in your chest and abdomen, not in your blood or in your marrow. I believe that you can be cured."

The head of the medical team came in while I was eating dinner Friday. "We'll start your chemo Monday, Mr. Jordan."

"Do we have to wait?"

The doctor said that he was on duty Saturday and that we could do the first cycle then.

"Tomorrow is your birthday," Dorothy protested.

I gave her hand a squeeze and smiled. I thought about the cancer cells racing around my body while I ate birthday cake. I had no intention of giving my body the weekend off.

"Let's get started with it," I said, trying to sound brave about something that I didn't feel very brave about.

CHEMOTHERAPY

By random selection, it was determined that I would receive the PROMACE-CYTOBOM protocol, which was being tested in clinical trials against standard protocols in treating lymphomas. There were eight drugs in this protocol that would have some different and hopefully fatal impact on cancer cells. The good news was that by using them together in combination, there was a greater chance that they would kill all the cancer cells before any of the cells developed resistance to the drugs. The bad news was that in the course of killing the cancer cells, they also kill your body's healthy cells and are particularly rough on your blood components.

Because I had an aggressive lymphoma, my cells were dividing rapidly and were peculiarly vulnerable to chemotherapy. This meant that if the chemo worked at all, it could work dramatically.

The doctor told me that he would give me "almost lethal" doses of the drugs in order to kill the cancer and that he was willing to deal with any complications and side effects that might develop.

A doctor friend had given me a lecture on chemotherapy before I had left Atlanta. "If you expect to get sick from your chemo, you will get very sick. Do not assume the worst . . . prepare for the worst, but hope for the best."

In the abstract, it sounded good, but I was scared to death of these powerful drugs. I had seen too many cancer patients wandering the halls, stopping to use their plastic nausea trays. I had heard stories of people who developed "anticipatory nausea," who threw up when they drove by the clinic just at the thought of their chemo, and horror stories of people who vomited for days after each treatment.

My primary doctor brought me the consent forms to sign before I took my chemo. "Before you sign, I have to inform you of potential side effects and risks. You want generalities or details?"

"I had rather have the details so I can spot any side effects," I said.

"On day one through day fourteen, you will take prednisone. It is a steroid. It will cause some redistribution in your body fat, can cause mood swings, and will increase your appetite."

"What are mood swings?"

"You might feel depressed one hour and exhilarated the next. We had one patient on prednisone who thought he was Jesus Christ!"

He continued. "On day one, you will get the following drugs intravenously: adriamycin, cytoxan, and VP-16. Adriamycin causes vomiting, hair loss and is harmful to your bone marrow. It can cause heart and liver damage but you will be closely monitored.

"Cytoxin causes nausea, hair loss, mouth ulcers, frequent urination, bladder irritation, and sometimes skin discoloration.

"On day eight, you will receive your second cycle of four drugs: vincristine, ARA-C, Bleomycin and Methotrexate. Bleomycin causes nausea, hair loss, bone marrow damage and can cause lung damage, although this is not common.

"Vincristine usually results in constipation and hair loss. You may experience 'neuropathies,' which will include jaw pain and numbness or cramps in your fingers and toes."

"Great," I said sarcastically.

"ARA-C causes. . . ."

"Enough!" I said, holding up my hand. "I've heard enough. All this is doing is scaring me. Are these drugs going to kill me or kill my cancer . . . or both?" I added as an afterthought.

"Mr. Jordan, they are going to kill your cancer for sure. The challenge is for them to kill every bit of your cancer, every cell . . . to leave the cancer so weakened that it can be cleaned up by your immune system. Along the way, they are going to play hell with your body and push it to the very limits, but we will monitor you very, very closely and deal with any problems that arise."

"Let's get started," I said as I signed the consent form and handed it back.

In a few minutes, the nurses had given me the anti-nausea drugs and had begun to give me intravenously the first "cycle" of the experimental protocol.

My favorite doctor walked into my room, smiled, and said, "Happy Birthday!"

I forced a smile. "Thanks for the presents," I said, nodding toward the IV.

He put his hand on my shoulder and squeezed me. "Mr. Jordan, I believe you are going to have many, many more birthdays."

"Do you really think so, doctor?"

"I really think so . . . and it is important that you think so too."

Although I felt wiped out and was heavily sedated from the drugs, the nausea never came. I waited and waited to be sick but instead felt better and better. My nurses were surprised.

"Unbelievable," a large, jolly nurse said. "You've got an iron stomach, Mr. Jordan."

By six o'clock, I was eating yogurt, calling my mother and siblings and celebrating my first treatment without horrible side effects.

Dorothy finally left the hospital after ten. I was exhilarated to be feeling good and had trouble sleeping. When no one was looking, I walked outside the hospital to enjoy the crisp breeze and clear fall sky. It was invigorating. I had dodged a bullet that day and was grateful. I wondered how much of it was just dumb luck and how much of it had been my determination not be to sick.

LIVING WITH CANCER

With the first treatment behind us, Dorothy and I tried to develop a normal routine and focus on life in the present tense. It was not easy; there was always something to do medically that reminded me that I had cancer. I had to take several different medicines every morning and evening. I had to take my temperature four times a day to spot any signs of early infection. I had to rinse my mouth out with a special preparation six times a day to reduce the occurrence of mouth sores and fever blisters, and I had to apply a special fluoride treatment to my teeth each night to ward off the decay that was aggravated by the chemo. Sleep was precious as bladder irritation caused me to get up every hour or so during the night.

All of these little medical chores cumulatively did not take more than an hour a day, but they were a constant reminder of my illness. In addition, there were always two or three visits to the hospital each week for blood counts, X rays, and chemo treatments. I realized that having cancer could become your full-time job and preoccupation. But I was determined not to let this happen.

I started to focus on my work and found that I could still be productive. I could even — for periods of time — put the disease out of my mind. The chemotherapy had reduced my energy level to 30 to 40 percent, but on most days I felt pretty good. I started back jogging the day after my first treatment and got up to two or three miles a day. The fact that I could get out and do this, feel the wind against my face and sweat on my brow, gave me an enormous lift.

With my chemo treatments now scheduled on a regular basis, Dorothy and I worked hard to develop a routine and make a normal home life for Hamilton Jr. We took regular trips to the zoo and savored visits from our families. Dorothy resumed her jogging, went to great lengths to cook me nutritious and healthy meals at those odd hours of the day and the night when I did have an appetite. Most importantly, she was my cheer-leader and best friend. After a few months, our cozy Bethesda rental started to feel like home, and things seemed pretty normal.

But things were not normal.

I knew that I was receiving the best medical treatment in the world at NCI. But after the first cycle of chemotherapy was completed, I realized that while the doctors were doing great things for my body, they were doing nothing for my mind. And I understood why.

At a major research center where doctors are treating very sick patients and testing new protocols, there is little time left to worry about a patient's emotional condition. In the abstract, they all understand the benefits of a positive attitude, but there are not enough hours in the day to play doctor and therapist. And even when acknowledging the importance of the right attitude, their advice is superficial.

"Have a positive attitude," one young doctor suggested during a check-up. When I asked him what he meant, he said, "Just hang on!"

I was not content to just "hang on." I believed that there was much I could do to assist in a return to good health. But I realized ultimately that I would have to look inside myself to find the emotional and spiritual resources necessary to develop and sustain a positive attitude.

An obvious starting point was to talk to other cancer patients. They — not my doctors and nurses — were the ones who really understood what I was going through.

Some patients were withdrawn, depressed, and didn't even want to talk. One man about my age simply cut me off when I asked about his cancer: "Look, I've got my problems and you've got yours . . . just leave me alone! I don't want to talk to anybody."

But there were others who were talkative, laughing, and extroverted. One little old lady of about seventy kept me in stitches for about fifteen minutes with jokes about doctors and death. When she ran out of cancer jokes, she started in with some dirty jokes chock-full of four-letter words that could have been told in a Las Vegas nightclub. She cleared the area where we were sitting and talking.

I found this second group of patients had come to grips with their disease and the realities of cancer despite — in many cases — poor prognoses. In more cases than not, these people were doing well medically and exceeding their doctors' expectations.

I got one doctor who was treating me to talk about the impact of attitude on disease. "Look," he said, "you have two cancer patients with the same disease and the same prognosis. One goes home, cuts himself off from family and friends, locks himself in a room watching television, expects to die and does die. The other surrounds herself with the love and support of family and friends, continues working, is determined to beat cancer, and either does beat it or greatly exceeds the medical prognosis. Doctors know this anecdotally and know it instinctively. The problem is that we have trouble dealing with anything that we can't prove or quantify. Most of us just don't have time to think about this stuff."

As I talked to more and more cancer patients who exhibited this joy of life, I was inspired by their attitude . . . an attitude that I did not yet have. I gained a deeper understanding that theirs was not merely "a will to live." Many were in the late stages of their illness, were not expected to live or were being treated for rare diseases with highly experimental therapies because nothing else had worked. Although expressed in different ways, I heard the same thing time and again. They described their cancer as a "strange blessing" that had "focused their life" or made them "appreciate life." They cherished each day, every friend, and each gesture of love or affection.

Some dwelled on the importance of a spouse or loved one. Most mentioned religious faith. Several recommended particular books.

I went to the store and bought so many books that I carried them out to my car in a grocery cart. Some were goofy, others relied totally on prayer, and still others recommended untested diets or vitamins. I read ten or fifteen pages before putting most of them aside.

But two authors — Norman Cousins and Dr. Carl Simonton — have written books about the mind-body relationship that opened my mind to thinking about my illness in a totally different light. Both authors are grounded in practical knowledge, but with a healthy respect for things that we know but cannot necessarily prove.

Norman Cousins, a layman, wrote in *Anatomy of an Illness* how he refused to accept his doctor's death sentence for a bizarre degenerative disease. He described how he fought back, designed his own "treatment," and over a period of time was returned to full and normal health.

Dr. Carl Simonton, a radiation oncologist, had worked for twenty-five years to understand the impact of attitude on cancer. His book, *Getting Well Again*, is an inspiration for anyone with cancer.

The theme of both books is that the natural state of the human body is good health and that the body contains enormously effective natural healing powers which can be employed to beat disease. Indeed, every day, the human body's natural system kills germs, viruses, and cancer cells run amok. Both Cousins and Simonton believe — based on personal experience and years of study — that a person can help to muster these powers, and that a person's belief in the natural healing power of the human body can have a significant impact on the course of cancer.

These books said, in essence, that just because we do not understand how something works does not mean that it does not work. The medical profession has a name for the impact of a person's belief on the course of an illness — they call it the "placebo effect." It seemed strange that many in the medical profession can accept the reality of the "placebo effect" while distrusting theories and studies based on that same phenomenon.

Both authors strongly recommended that cancer patients work in active partnership with their health team, emphasizing the importance of attitude, stress reduction, exercise, diet, and the happiness that comes naturally from family and friends. Above all, they recommended that a person must have a purpose in life beyond their own narrow and selfish desire to survive.

These books became very important to Dorothy and me. Not because they contained some easy "secret cure," but because they were compatible with our own values and beliefs. I believe in a kind and benevolent God, but I have always felt that God helps those who help themselves. I cannot expect God to fight this battle for me alone — I must do my part. Sure, God is capable of miracles, but it is unlikely that he will waste one on me.

These authors provided me an intellectual framework to think about my cancer differently. I began to regard my body as a battlefield for the war being waged between the cancer cells and the chemotherapy. It was my job to keep my body — and mind — healthy and positive. Some mornings I would literally roll out of bed onto the floor because I did not have the energy to stand up. Eventually, however, I would stand up, and no matter how weak I felt, I would walk or even jog a couple of miles every day. And without exception, that exercise, that attempt at being normal gave me energy and hope to keep going.

I began to see for the first time that this ordeal could be the basis for refocusing my own life. Cancer does not have to be a curse . . . it can be an opportunity to gain insight into your life.

Once I believed that emotionally, spiritually, and intellectually, I could undergo anything . . . and was prepared for any outcome.

My remaining treatments went well but were not easy. Over the long haul, the powerful chemicals had a cumulative, debilitating effect on my body. Because my white blood cell "count" (which is the essence of the immune system) stayed surprisingly high, I asked my doctors to increase my dosage on the accepted theory that the more your body can tolerate, the better. After much internal debate — and my signing an entire new set of forms — they gave me the increased dosage for the last two months.

CHEMO CARRIES ME BACK TO OLD SAIGON

"Just relax," the nurse said reassuringly, patting my arm as she guided me down into the brown leather recliner in the "chemo room," the playful yellow and blue walls punctuated by a number of what the staff called "stations." Each station was a serious-looking reclining chair surrounded by bottles — full of colorful poisons — sitting atop tall, shiny rods on rollers and tethered by long tubes to the arms of patients.

On my first visit, she had pulled out a card and said, "I am going to read you your rights . . . ha, ha!" — then read in a quiet voice the different drugs she was giving me and the risks involved:

"Adriamyecin can cause permanent damage to your heart and kidneys. . . ."

I glanced around the room . . . a couple of patients were dosing, others read and one fidgeted nervously as he watched the drip . . . drip . . . drip of the liquid into the clear tube taped to his pale, bony arm.

"Vincristine can cause permanent nerve damage, including neuropathies. . . ."

I signed the release and watched closely as she tied the rubber strap around my arm and poked around for a vein in which to insert the large needle.

She chatted nonstop, her commentary spiced with one-liners that were funny the first time. By the third visit, I had heard them all and had to force a smile or slight chuckle to acknowledge her effort.

I realized over time that — like most of the medical staff at the National Cancer Institute — her chatter was nothing more than a defense mechanism. While at one level, she was certainly "connecting" to her patients, her constant blabber protected her from real conversation and from getting emotionally involved with the endless stream of poor souls that came her way. I couldn't really blame her; so many of the cancer patients who showed up at NCI had failed first- and even second-line therapies elsewhere and had come there to take their last, best shot.

She started me with an antinausea drip, which made me drowsy, before she began to feed in the five drugs in my experimental protocol. I hated the feeling that followed as the grogginess spread over my body; I felt punchy and was no longer clearheaded or in control.

I had tried reading, which never worked, and sometimes closed my eyes and pretended to sleep just to avoid having to talk to the nurses.

I told myself over and over again that it was wasted energy to try to wonder how I had contracted this disease. I fought it and rarely thought about it — except when I was taking my chemo and would find my mind drifting to the hidden origins of my illness and remembering Vietnam. . . .

I thought about those long, hot, and humid, days in a small town in the Mekong Delta called Tan An, life with the Vietnamese family where I was in language training, the bowls full of rice and vegetables — occasionally augmented with a piece of tough, barely chewable "beef," which — having "gone native" — I struggled to master with the chopsticks. After I learned that dog meat was a Vietnamese delicacy, I made a point of avoiding all meats.

I could remember like it was yesterday watching Ba Chu, the old grandmother, teeth black from eating betel nut, sitting in the open yard scrubbing the vegetables that would later be sold to the stands along the road, complaining nonstop about the "American poison" that had ruined the field where her family rented land and grew their precious vegetables.

Everyone in the village had a different story, but it turned out that on two or three occasions low-flying American planes had dropped some kind of herbicide on the thick jungle which ran along the river in an effort to "defoliate" areas where the Viet Cong were thought to be hiding at night.

The spray didn't kill any VC but seemed to have destroyed broad swaths of crops in the nearby fields. The angry villagers complained to their local officials that the Americans were destroying their livelihood. The "official response" was that the wind had blown the spray intended for the nearby jungle over onto the crops.

The villagers didn't care about the intentions . . . all they knew was that a lot of their crops had been destroyed.

During the first few weeks there, we met a few young U.S. military officers who were intrigued with Americans not in the military. They listened skeptically to our "mission" and — like many of the Vietnamese — suspected that we worked for the CIA. We wrangled a chopper ride from them, which allowed us to see the Mekong Delta from the air and to witness part of the "pacification" effort. On that day the effort amounted to our flying at several thousand feet over what they called "hostile populations" and hand-throwing cartoon-style leaflets from the helicopter that said, in essence, that the Saigon government and their allies — the U.S. military — were the good guys and the Viet Cong were the bad guys.

From several thousand feet or so, one of the young officers pointed out brown spots where the "herbicide" had been sprayed in an otherwise lush, green countryside.

"The stuff the Air Force sprays is ba-a-a-d stuff . . . it'll kill anything!"

The Vietnamese family I was living with told us that the leaflets we had seen dropped were very useful — as toilet paper for the rural Vietnamese.

It was years later before I would understand that this herbicide, containing dioxin, had been widely sprayed all over South Vietnam and that it was called Agent Orange because of the orange-colored bands around the 55-gallon drums containing the chemical spray. In what the U.S. Air Force designated "Operation Ranch Hand," an estimated one-tenth of the total land mass of South Vietnam, or about sixty-six hundred square miles, were sprayed with Agent Orange, 1967–69 being the years of highest activity and volume.

Because the low altitudes at which they flew exposed them to small-arms fire, the "Operation Ranch Hand" crews were the most highly decorated air units in the war.

After a number of scientific protests, the United States ceased to use Agent Orange in 1970. Years later, veterans — who were showing up with inordinate numbers of neuropathies and certain types of cancer — began to demand investigation by the U.S. government.

STOPPING COMMUNISM IN ASIA

It was not the way I had planned to arrive in Vietnam. After the long stuffy flight from Manila, I hurried off the plane and ducked into the dingy, humid bathroom in the Saigon airport, barely lit by a single bulb hanging from a cord. When I started to urinate, I felt an intense burning — like someone had set my crotch on fire. I had never felt a pain like that before and understood what it meant to "climb the wall." I had a sinking feeling that the innocent-looking young Filipino girl at the International Voluntary Services "going away" party in Manila was not so innocent after all.

I went "cold turkey," didn't drink another thing to avoid urinating. After a long wait going through customs, I found my way to a military compound and a smart-ass Army doctor.

"Welcome to Vi-e-t Nam, Mr. Jordan," he said sarcastically after looking at my urine under a slide. "Congratulations. It takes most guys a few weeks or months . . . you set some kind of record by arriving here with a first-class case of the clap."

I was embarrassed to death. I had never had any kind of venereal disease before and felt filthy all over. My first reaction was to take a hot shower and burn my clothes. The crazy thought crossed my mind that this would be reported home, but I said to myself, "Hell, I'm an adult, twenty-two years old, and halfway around the world . . . they are not going to write my parents!"

All such thoughts vanished as he pulled out a needle big enough for a horse, made me bend over and stuck it in my buttocks. He seemed to enjoy my discomfort.

My noble mission to Vietnam had begun on a low and humiliating note.

"What are you? CIA or what?"

Trying to recover some of my dignity, I said in my most serious voice, "I am a civilian volunteer. I am going to work in refugee relocation."

"Whaddaya mean, volunteer?"

"Well, I volunteered to come here."

"What are you getting, thirty, forty thou a year?"

"I make $120 a month," I responded proudly.

"Bullshit! You are either lying or crazy! Or both. And if you are telling me the truth, you need to go down the hall and see a shrink . . . nobody volunteers for this place. Vietnam is the asshole of the world!"

While many other young Americans had powerful reasons to go or not to go to Vietnam, my motivation was pretty simple — a sense of adventure. I had flat feet and a bad knee, which earned me a medical deferment from the draft, but I had a feeling that something important was happening in that distant place, and I wanted to see it firsthand.

However, when people asked why in the hell I was going "over there," *adventure* was not a very good answer. So I hid behind the more noble cause of "supporting my country." It was years later before I could admit to myself what a foolish and dangerous decision I had made.

But going into my junior year at the University of Georgia, I had no idea what I would do after graduation. The expectation of my family — with attorneys on both sides — was that I would practice law. I worked as an orderly at a hospital my junior year and senior year and enjoyed my lowly job making life just a little better for my patients. But I ended up with neither the desire to be a lawyer nor the grades to go to medical school. That's when I started thinking about going to Vietnam.

The antiwar movement had not penetrated the "juke-box room" at my fraternity house at the University of Georgia, where the brothers started gathering in the early afternoon every day to drink beer, swap stories, and sing along to "Louie-Lou-ee, Ooo-ooo . . . shake-o your thang!"

I had two types of friends. Some were in ROTC, the guys who dressed up in their uniforms a couple of times a week, marched around the campus, and played sol-dier. The others were the guys who — through their families or political connections — got into the National Guard summer programs ("Army Lite"), which required six weeks of basic training and sentenced them to once-a-month weekend duty for a couple of years and pretty much guaranteed that they would not be sent overseas. "The Viet Cong would have to be invading Miami before any of us get called up to active duty," one frat brother explained. The Guard was "a royal pain in the ass, but better than being shot in the ass in Nam."

I suppose there was the third type — students who were against the war, but none were visible at UGA, or else they were too smart to reveal their true feelings.

Then I read a magazine article about an organization called IVS (International Voluntary Services), which had operated since 1954. For very little pay, young people were assigned to work in third-world countries doing "community development" and agriculture work.

Described by the writer as the "Peace Corps" of Vietnam, the IVS was showing the Vietnamese people the "human face" of U.S. concern and were making their own special contribution to the effort. I was intrigued by the article and privately found it exciting and romantic. I fancied myself as a kind of "junior diplomat" for my country, doing my patriotic duty in this faraway and dangerous place.

My parents saw nothing good in this new idea and argued strenuously against my going. Nevertheless, while my mother cried at the airport and my father dabbed at his eyes with the white handkerchief he always wore in his suit pocket, I also knew that they took a certain amount of pride in my volunteering to go when so many others were going to great lengths to avoid military service at all costs.

I had bought myself a dark suit with thin gray stripes, a red tie, and some new black shoes and showed up at a Harpers Ferry, West Virginia, hotel for the two-week

"Ambassador Jordan"

IVS "indoctrination" before going to the Philippines for language training.

I arrived a bit early at the hotel to find a scruffy-looking bunch of people with long hair milling around, and I wondered where my group was meeting. But when I began to notice that several of these folks had on IVS "Hello" nametags, I realized that this was indeed my IVS "class." So there I was . . . standing there in the middle of a bunch of hippies with my pin-striped suit on. A few were friendly, others were not.

I started to meet them and learned their stories . . . they went to schools like Berkeley, Harvard, and Goshen. After a long and boring welcome and lecture on the history of IVS, a small group gathered on the porch after dinner, talking quietly among themselves and passing around cigarettes.

As I walked up, one of the guys asked, "Want a drag?" and stuck a foul-smelling little cigarette in my face.

Taken aback, I held up my hand and said. "No, no, no . . . I don't smoke."

"'Ambassador Jordan' does not smoke," someone snickered sarcastically. The entire group laughed . . . but the name stuck for a while.

As I smelled the weird odor from the smoke and heard the wisecracks, I finally realized that I had been offered pot.

TAN AN, SOUTH VIETNAM

My initial IVS "training" assignment in South Vietnam was intense language study while living with a Vietnamese family in the Mekong Delta. A teacher would come in during the morning and we would work for hours on pronunciation and vocabulary. Vietnamese is a very difficult tonal language where the same word said five different ways has five totally different meanings. There were a few in our group who "got it," but most of my colleagues and I struggled with the language, constantly trying it on the Vietnamese family with whom we lived and at the little roadside stands that sold fresh pineapple and warm Cokes.

Our little house sat off the main road to Saigon, and during the day U.S. and ARVN troops moved freely up and down the road. But at night, the Viet Cong ruled. We lived right on the river, and every night we went to sleep to the sound of the choppers as they meandered up and down the waterway using infrared technology, hoping to catch small groups of VC moving through the darkness.

I began doing refugee work in the Mekong Delta, trying to relocate vegetable farmers from the highlands of Vietnam whose villages had been taken over by the Viet Cong. And I — a twenty-three-year-old American who spoke about fifty words of Vietnamese and had never grown anything other than a mild beard — was supposed to help these lifelong farmers learn to grow rice.

RICE FARMING IN VIETNAM

I began to spend a lot of time at night reading books on the history of Vietnam. Quickly I came to view the ongoing conflict from a slightly different perspective. For over six hundred years, the Vietnamese people had been fighting their Chinese neighbors and later the colonial French, whom they finally drove out of Vietnam in 1954. We seemed merely to be the next group of foreigners passing through, fighting for objectives that the people neither understood nor shared. And we were supporting a corrupt military government that lacked the popular support of the Vietnamese people.

I knew that our nation's goals were noble in Vietnam and certainly seemed so to those in the White House. It was pretty simple: We were trying to "halt" communism in Southeast Asia and bring democracy to Vietnam.

But it seemed a lot to expect that the Vietnamese people — who had been fighting "foreign devils" for generations — would understand or appreciate what our country was doing. Why were the Americans any different from the Chinese or the French who brought war and devastation to their villages, destroyed their rice fields, and killed their sons and daughters?

Certainly, through their eyes, we were no different.

In early December 1967, I developed a stiff neck followed by a violent fever. When I finally got a thermometer, I realized from my hospital work that my fever — sometimes 105 or 106 — was dangerously high. After lying in my bed for several days, sweating and sleeping and sometimes delirious, the family that I was living with sent for an IVS volunteer in a nearby town.

Stu Bloch, Harvard '67, a loud-mouthed, wise-cracking radical who had been unmerciful in ribbing me, turned out to be my true friend. He found a small wagon, laid me on it with a pillow and blanket, and pulled me several miles to a local U.S. military post, where I was put in a jeep and driven to Cam Ranh Bay, the largest U.S. military base in Vietnam and immediately admitted to the military hospital and moved to an isolation ward.

CHRISTMAS AT CAM RANH BAY, SOUTH VIETNAM, 1967

"Oh my God . . . he's coming here! Can you believe it? He's coming here . . . the president is coming to our unit!" shouted one of the male nurses, waking me from a deep afternoon sleep.

All of a sudden, the long, low quonset hut that had been turned into a hospital ward with about thirty beds was a beehive of activity as nurses and orderlies emptied trash baskets, picked up around the beds, and buttoned their uniforms.

It took me a couple of minutes to find out what was happening, but I soon figured out that President Lyndon Johnson — returning from a trip to the funeral of Australian Prime Minister Harold Holt — had decided to pay a Christmas visit to "see his boys" by visiting our hospital.

By this time I had been in the hospital for three weeks, my illness still undiagnosed. Now not just my neck but my entire upper body was bent over in stiffness. The air force doctors initially thought it was some strange form of meningitis, but they were not sure and chalked it up to just one more strange tropical disease. The first week or ten days I had been heavily sedated and could barely remember my time in the isolation ward.

But once it was determined that I was not contagious and had begun to respond to a battery of antibiotics, I was moved to a regular ward. I was still sick and heavily medicated, and like clockwork — every four to six hours — my fever would shoot up and this huge knot (the size of a large lemon) would well up on the back of my neck.

While in pain and sedated, I was not so sick that I didn't realize that the soldiers around me quickly figured out I was not one of them, but a civilian "volunteer" — something they could not even comprehend. Neither brave nor a fool, I didn't even try to explain IVS . . . maybe they would think that I was an intelligence agent.

Our ward was a mixture of guys . . . a few recovering from battle wounds and surgery, others like myself who had malaria or other strange tropical diseases that they simply called malaria. A handful of the guys had developed a strain of gonorrhea that did not responded to penicillin or any other drug. Their situation had stabilized and was under control, but they were still "sexually contagious." These poor saps were not going to be allowed to return to the States until they were "clean."

As these guys were "long-timers," who weren't acutely sick and knew all the ropes, they tended to have the run of our ward. Their leader was a loud-mouthed marine named Grimes, whom everyone called "Grimey" — not a term of affection but an accurate description of his coarse appearance and foul mouth. Short and built like a tank, Grimey acted like he was in charge of our ward, and at some level he probably was.

One morning early in my hospital stay when I was having a difficult time even moving my upper body, Grimey jumped on top of my chest, pinned my shoulders down with his knees, and yelled out, "Okay, Georgee-boy . . . tell us why you volunteered to come to this shit hole? You're not a really a volunteer, are you? Betcha you're a rich spy or CIA? Or maybe just a queer? I bet you are a queer . . . I've got something for you to eat that's better than that crap they serve here. Want it? Do you want it, Georgee-boy? I bet you do!"

Although on my back with the big marine sitting on my chest, I tried to hit him with my good left arm, but I telegraphed my feeble half-swing, and he easily deflected it.

"Oh . . . Georgee-boy wants to fight?" he mocked as he started to playfully slap my face with his open palms, then slapped me a few times really hard. He finally balled one fist and delivered a serious punch which glanced off my nose and hit my eye. I started to cuss him and struggled to get up when a large pair of black hands encircled the marine's neck from behind, literally lifted Grimes up in the air and threw him onto the floor.

I knew it was Willie Roberts, a black air force orderly from Bainbridge, Georgia, about sixty miles from my hometown of Albany, Georgia. A huge, soft-spoken man who carried himself with great dignity, Willie had changed my bed when I was unable to move and had brought me rags with ice to break my fever. We had long conversations about family back home or about his shopping trips to "Aw-benny" when he was a boy.

Grimey now found himself on the floor, with Willie sitting on his chest, his hands tightly gripping the marine's bulging red neck. Grimey was flailing his arms wildly when Willie got right in his face and said in a low voice, "You chicken-shit marine, next time I catch you messing with my sick Georgia buddy, I'm gonna whup yo ass, understand! I gonna wipe this floor with your ugly face, understand? Do you understand?"

Grimey's beet-red face shook up and down until Willie let him go. He lay on the floor for another minute or so, his chest heaving up and down, breathing heavily. He glared at me as he pulled himself to his feet, and the small crowd that had gathered drifted away.

I waited in fear for the next few days for Grimey to exact his revenge when Willie was off-duty. But Grimey never said another word to me, and his reign over our ward came to a crashing end. For the rest of my stay, he kept to himself and his few marine buddies and was ignored by the rest of the ward.

Life was easier for me as I began to recover.

Suddenly, the quonset hut door flew open and the president's entourage entered — Johnson towering above them, with large, almost floppy ears, and dressed in khakis and a tan shirt covered with a flak jacket. Johnson was bigger than I expected and moved easily and quickly and with purpose. When he stopped to talk or shake hands, he seemed to pull the person toward him at the same time or to bend over for those too sick to sit up. The effect was that the soldiers had the president of the United States right in their face.

He worked the quonset hut like he might have worked a crowd of voters, moving at lightning speed down the long row of beds — waving to one, shouting a greeting to another, flashing a smile, and stopping at each fifth or sixth bed. Occasionally — when directed by the docs — he would pin a purple heart on the wounded soldiers . . . and in one case a medal for bravery.

When the president was three or four beds away, he caught my eye and appeared to be moving in my direction.

"Where you from, soldier?" he shouted out.

"Georgia," I said proudly.

Johnson started to smile when suddenly Grimey yelled out, "He's not a soldier, Mr. President. He's a peacenik!"

Johnson's head jerked back like I was a leper; he turned to the air force doc in charge, who whispered something into the president's large ear. He must have confirmed I was not a soldier as Johnson's exaggerated smile turned to rows of unhappy wrinkles. He glared at me for an instant and quickly moved to the bed across the aisle.

I felt both humiliated and cheated . . . I had planned to tell him about my Georgia roots and about working in Washington as an intern for his old friend, Senator Richard Russell, but I was dumbstruck and just sat there as the parade moved on. My once-in-a-lifetime chance to actually meet a president had been ruined by some jerk with a big mouth. I was devastated and fought back tears.

I left the hospital at Cam Ranh Bay a few weeks later. The huge knot on the back of my neck had marched up and down for several weeks, and finally — after a sustained assault of new antibiotics — it gradually disappeared. The red-headed air force doctor told me, "I don't know what in the hell it was . . . whatever it was, we probably don't even have a name for it in American medicine. I'm going to put it down as 'dengue fever.'"

He sent me to Saigon with strict orders to take it easy for a few weeks before I returned to my assignment in the mountains near Nha Trang. I was too weak to do anything so I hung around the IVS house practicing my

RECOVERING FROM "DENGUE FEVER," CAM RAHN BAY HOSPITAL

Vietnamese with a young teacher who came to the house to coach anyone who needed language help. I certainly qualified.

On the eve of Tet, the Vietnamese New Year, we awoke in the middle of the night to the noise of shelling, which we assumed was directed at the air base not far away. But soon we heard small-arms fire in the street, and we began to "feel" the shells as they literally shook our house, the lights flickering off and on.

Although we had no sense of it then, the Tet Offensive — which would mark the turning point in the war — had begun.

The IVS veterans at our house — some of whom were ten-year Vietnam veterans — recognized that this was more than just random shelling and quickly agreed that a houseful of Americans in the middle of Saigon could be a prime target for the Viet Cong. Using flashlights, we were led quickly through the narrow streets that night to nearby houses, and I hid under the bed of a tiny house until the heavy shelling ended the next morning and the gunfire became sporadic.

Back at the IVS house, we heard over the Armed Forces Radio Network that the Viet Cong had launched a well-coordinated offensive all over the country, making a mockery of the U.S. claim that we were winning "the hearts and minds" of the Vietnamese people. Indeed, the Tet Offensive demonstrated that the Viet Cong could strike at will — whenever and wherever they wanted to — even in the capital city.

A few days later, we got reports that a couple of IVS volunteers were missing and believed to be captured and that one, a conscientious objector, had been killed. I was sure that the Viet Cong assumed that any Americans mingling with the people and attempting to speak the language were "CIA."

It was a cruel irony . . . conscientious objectors half way around the world trying to help war victims had been killed in the very conflict they had opposed. Just as there was no good way for the American GIs to tell the difference between a friendly boy running along-side their tank and a Viet Cong prepared to toss a grenade down the hatch, we could hardly expect the Viet Cong to know the difference between GIs, intelligence agents, and do-gooders.

In the aftermath of the Tet offensive, IVS offered to cancel the contracts of its volunteers. A few stayed, but many went home.

I was confused, scared, and ready to leave.

The hospital stay and the Tet Offensive had wrung all of the romance out of Vietnam for me. I realized that I had flirted with death and that no American in Vietnam was safe anywhere . . . from germs or from bullets.

I did not want to die in that distant land for a cause I did not understand and for a reason I could not even articulate. The war permeated every aspect of life in South Vietnam. I concluded it was impossible for a white American to have a significant impact helping these people. We could be in the villages each day, struggling to speak their language, eating their rice, and making tiny steps toward what the pacification experts called "community development." But at night the Viet Cong would return with a nationalistic message, rice, and weapons. It was no contest.

At best, we were a symbol of our country's good intentions. At worst, in the minds of many Vietnamese, we had become the enemy, the reason for the killings, the destruction of their crops, the suffering.

Not many had the chance to leave as I did. Not the young men drafted, trained, and dumped into the middle of this strange war. Not the Vietnamese people who had been fighting foreign invaders for the past six hundred years. Nor the tens of millions of Vietnamese people who had no particular political ideology and only wanted to be left alone to live in peace and to grow their rice and vegetables.

The reaction to my coming home was disappointing in every respect. I thought that people might thank me for my attempted service.

Those who were "hawks" only knew that I had gone over as a civilian, had come home early, and had not been in the military. Those few who were beginning to question U.S. involvement or were against the war only knew that I had been in Vietnam with some government agency. When I came home to Georgia and had time to clear my head, I was sure that my country — with the very best intentions — had made a huge mistake in undertaking what President Eisenhower had warned against — a land war in Asia. Most importantly, we had confused nationalism with Communism and had allowed our obsession with Communism to drag us into the wrong war in the wrong place for the wrong reasons.

As one general said, "The only way to win the war is to destroy Vietnam." Based on my short time there, that is exactly what we had tried to do . . . but we had neither destroyed Vietnam nor won the war.

I kept looking for black-and-white answers in Vietnam — a way to reconcile our good intentions with the mess that had been created — and all I could see were shades of gray.

Lying there in the chemo room at NCI, I watched the slow drip . . . drip . . . drip of the clear liquid that I hoped would save my life. As I watched the liquid move in fits and starts down the tube enroute to my arm, I realized that neither Vietnam nor cancer made much sense.

Our country had lost one war where I was nothing more than a bystander. Now I was as totally involved as one could be in a battle for my own life.

I wondered if I would win.

NCI, ROY COHN, AND D.C. DAYS

Several months later, I was at NCI for a checkup, and, while feeling my stomach for possible enlarged lymph nodes, one of my favorite young clinicians teased me by saying, "You're not the only big shot around here."

"Former big shot," I said, trying to sound uninterested. I assumed he was talking about the famous Washington attorney Edward Bennett Williams, who was being treated at NCI while bravely battling colon cancer. I had bumped into him on several occasions in the chemo room.

"Yep, this guy was really big, but long before your time . . . Roy Cohn. You know who he was, don't you?"

I almost fell off the table. I knew him only too well. Unfortunately, he was not before my time. In fact, he had successfully smeared me just as he had many others in a long and controversial career that started as Joe McCarthy's henchman back in his red-baiting days in the early 1950s.

"What the hell is Roy Cohn doing here?"

"Officially, he is here for cancer," he said sarcastically, "But we are treating him for advanced AIDS, which he denies that he has."

It did not surprise me that this man, whose reputation and public image had been built on lies, might die living one.

———————

I had never met Roy Cohn, but I felt like I knew him. I remembered seeing old news clips of Cohn sitting at Senator Joseph McCarthy's side during the hearings which bore his name, whispering in his ear with tidbits and cues, which the Senator used to paint good and often innocent people as "Communist sympathizers" and "reds." I remembered the riveting response of Joseph Welsh, General Counsel for the U.S. Army, who was defending a young associate (Fred Fisher) whom McCarthy and Cohn were attempting to smear:

> Senator, I have ceased to be surprised by your reckless conduct and your willingness to stoop to any level to smear innocent people. Let us not

assassinate this lad further, Senator.
You have done enough. Have you no
decency, sir, at long last? Have you no
sense of decency?

That exchange in 1954 began to turn the tide of public opinion against McCarthy and Cohn and marked the
beginning of the end for McCarthy's reign of terror, as
more and more good people stood up to their bullying
tactics. McCarthy was quickly discredited and defeated,
and he died in 1957.

Roy Cohn never made a political comeback nation-
ally, but practiced law in New York City, cultivated
contacts with key members of the media, and would
pop up every now and then representing some
celebrity (like Donald Trump) in some highly public
divorce settlement or scandal.

It was an unbelievable irony that a quarter of a century later (1979) Roy Cohn could concoct a scandal
involving me and successfully sell it to the major news
organizations. Roy Cohn had shrewdly exploited my
vulnerability — my unattractive public image, which
had been largely created by the gossip columnists and
Washington pundits — for the benefit of his clients.

WUNDERKIND TO FOOL IN SIX SHORT MONTHS

When we arrived in Washington, I had been hailed as a political genius, but it did not take long for my reputation and image to be reduced to that of a cartoon character.

I thought about the long road to the White House, those hard years when I would drive the ex-governor of Georgia in my beat-up green VW to the Atlanta airport to catch a plane to New Hampshire or Iowa. In those days, our fledgling campaign could not afford two tickets, and Jimmy Carter would fly coach to Iowa or New Hampshire and be met by volunteers who would drive him around and put him up in their homes.

People didn't laugh at us openly, but some of our friends and even some members of my own family snickered at us behind our backs — a peanut farmer from Georgia running for president of the United States? Preposterous!

The only thing that kept me going through those years was the dream of Jimmy Carter's presidency and the possibility of changing politics in this country — challenging the status quo and shaking up the Washington political establishment, so out of touch with the mood and needs of the American people.

Working in the White House was never a goal of mine, but when I was offered the chance to go with the president-elect to Washington, I was caught up in the excitement of the moment and said "Yes" to that once-in-a-lifetime opportunity. I never wanted to be a public figure, and I certainly never dreamed that I would become a controversial figure and ultimately a political liability for the man and the cause that I served.

Because Jimmy Carter was not a product of Congress or well-known to the political establishment, there was an inordinate curiosity about him. As a result of their long years in Congress and Washington, Presidents Ford, Nixon, Johnson, and Kennedy were well-known to the press and to the movers and shakers in the Washington political establishment.

But Jimmy Carter was an enigma, and his success was both celebrated and resented by the Democratic establishment. It was bad enough that they did not know him or have any stake in his candidacy, but to make matters worse, Carter had defeated their own favorites — Morris Udall, Birch Bayh, Scoop Jackson, et al. — in political battles all over the country.

By the time we arrived in Washington, there was a strong but subtle feeling: "You guys from Georgia won the White House by running against Washington, through politician gimmickry and just plain dumb luck . . . but we are going to show you who is Boss in this town!"

As a result of Carter's unexpected success in the Democratic primaries, Jody Powell and I had the highest public profile among the people around Jimmy Carter. Jody was always at Carter's side and became a familiar and popular figure to the members of the national press who traveled with Carter and covered the

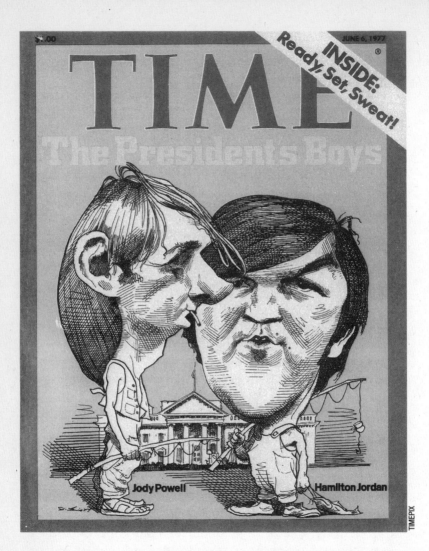

"FROM WUNDERKIND TO FOOL"

campaign. They appreciated Jody's quick mind, his access to the candidate, and his sharp wit. Initially, Jody was inaccurately perceived as playing the traditional and limited role of "mouthpiece." Over time, the press realized that Jody was a key influence on Carter as well.

Because I was the campaign manager and was given exaggerated credit for the campaign strategy that carried Carter to Washington, there was always great curiosity about me and my future role in the White House. I had never traveled with candidate Carter, and only rarely granted press interviews. . . . I figured it was my role to stay in the background and do my job. Consequently, I became a mystery to the national press corps.

After the general election, I worked closely with Carter and Fritz Mondale on the selection of the Cabinet, rarely granted interviews to the press, and ended up in the large corner office of recent chiefs-of-staff . . . even though we had vowed repeatedly throughout the campaign not to have a powerful chief-of-staff.

I realized that I was in trouble when I read an article in the *Washington Post* by Sally Quinn describing me as the "second-most powerful person in Washington."

"My God," I told Jody, "I've been set up for a great big fall!"

Even I could not imagine how big and how sudden my "fall" would be.

I had never been a public person and had trouble thinking of myself as one. I was wrong and naive in the extreme for failing to appreciate the fact that anyone who worked at the White House — and particularly someone like myself who had a long and close relationship with the president and worked in the office that had been occupied by Sherman Adams, Clarke Clifford, and H. R. Haldeman — was a highly public person, like it or not. And that public position carries with it certain responsibilities, including the need to be at least responsive if not proactive in dealing with the press. By shunning the national press in hopes of keeping a low profile, I instead helped to create an atmosphere that allowed a highly unattractive image of myself to be presented.

Despite the perception that developed of my being a playboy and a rube, I spent most of my first year physically at the White House, working fourteen and sixteen hours, seven days a week. I never went out socially and had no desire to be part of the Washington "scene." This was interpreted by many as a sign of my contempt, and one of the constant complaints about the "Georgia mafia" was that it was difficult to get them — "particularly Jordan" — to attend any of their gatherings.

Vice President Mondale — who had an office next to mine — had become a close friend and adviser. He was very much a part of the Washington establishment and strongly recommended that I "get out more" and let people get to know me.

I decided to attend a small dinner party given by Barbara Walters in honor of the Israeli and Egyptian ambassadors to celebrate progress made toward an

Israeli-Egyptian peace agreement. I was seated next to the Egyptian ambassador's wife at a table that included Henry Kissinger, humorist Art Buchwald, and ABC newsman Sam Donaldson. It was a typical dinner party with interesting people and congenial conversation. There were too many toasts, which made for a very long evening, but otherwise it was uneventful and enjoyable. I was glad to have gone and felt that I had at least begun to pay my dues to social Washington. Perhaps it would be another couple of months before I had to make an appearance at another one.

Several weeks after the dinner, a scathing article appeared in the "Style" section of the *Washington Post*, the theme of which was that the Carter people worked too hard, ignored the social mores of the Capital City, and were paying a big price politically for not being more a part of the cultural fabric of the city. And, of course, when the Carter people did socialize, they made fools of themselves.

The evidence cited was that when attending Barbara Walters's dinner for the Egyptian and Israeli ambassadors I had grabbed the bodice of the Egyptian ambassador's wife, peered down her dress, and declared loudly, "I have always wanted to see the pyramids!"

Because it appeared in the "Style" section of the *Post*, the reaction initially was not serious, and no one seemed too concerned about it. In fact, most people seemed to think that it was funny . . . except me, because I knew that nothing remotely like that had ever happened.

And it seemed to make absolutely no difference that I denied the story unequivocally, or that the Egyptian ambassador's wife, Mrs. Ghorbal — a lovely, matronly lady, old enough to be my grandmother — denied it emphatically or that every other person at our table denied seeing or hearing anything like the incident so vividly detailed in the *Post* article.

But the "pyramids" story just became part of my political biography and was accepted without question by others, adding to the litany of other funny and outrageous stories about me that started out in the gossip columns and soon gained momentum and credibility through their appearance in political columns or their mention on the television talk shows. Most of these stories were totally or largely untrue.

The muckraker Jack Anderson, for example, wrote that I and the president's close friend Charles Kirbo — himself a distinguished attorney — had taken a $10 million bribe from fugitive Robert Vesco to put the fix in for him with the Justice Department. Made up out of whole cloth, Anderson's story prompted a grand jury investigation that lasted almost a year just as another grand jury was organized to investigate alleged wrongdoings in the operation of the Carter Peanut Warehouse in Plains. (The special prosecutor concluded in his final report that "not one peanut" was missing.)

The last conversation that I had with my dear father — the night before he died — he was sobbing into the phone as he said, "Son, I just don't understand why those people up there don't just leave you alone?"

I put up a brave front, told people that it "came with the territory," but I was terribly embarrassed and hurt. Try as I could to laugh all of these stories off, I could not ignore the fact that I had quickly become defined — not by my actual work — but by these outrageous and largely inaccurate allegations.

As Jody was fond of saying, "The truth never, never catches up with the wild rumor or the interesting and funny gossip."

But when the FBI knocked on the door of my little apartment around 10:00 P.M. in August 1979, I was no longer able to dismiss it as gossip or as pundits taking potshots at me merely because I worked for the president.

While the FBI had interviewed me probably a half-dozen times regarding various charges made against members of our administration, this one seemed different — the call from the agent at night, the insistence that they interview me right away, and the refusal to discuss the reason.

The two agents who showed up at my apartment were polite but all business: "Anything that you say here can be used against you in a court of law . . . you have a right to an attorney. . . ."

I started squirming but tried to calm myself, thinking, "For God's sake, Hamilton, don't act like you have done anything wrong! How you react could determine whether these guys believe you or not."

Did I remember, they asked, being in New York with Jody Powell in the spring of 1978, and did I remember going to the fashionable New York City nightclub, Studio 54, with Jody?

I told them that I did remember going there briefly on one occasion, that I didn't remember the time or date, but that I did not remember Jody's being with me.

They asked me some more questions, and then showed me a series of pictures, and asked me to identify them. I told them that I did not know or remember any of the persons in the pictures.

Finally, the real purpose of their visit became crystal-clear: "Did you — while in Studio 54 on the occasion that you did visit — use the drug cocaine?"

I told them absolutely that I had not, that I had never, never used drugs and that people who knew me would confirm that. While I was still nervous at the idea of the FBI visit, I was actually relieved to learn how ridiculous the charge was and knew that no credible person anywhere could or would claim to having seen me use drugs. Ironically, I was considered hard-nosed and a "tiger" on drug use among people in the campaign and now in the White House. I was not naive as to what was going on socially in the late 1970s and the widespread recreational use of cocaine, but I had warned our young staff time and time again that drug use would simply not be tolerated. As I often said, "When you work in this building — the White House — you do not have the luxury to pick and choose which laws you will obey."

When I demanded the source of the story, they told me that two men, Steve Rubell and Ian Schrager, said that I used cocaine at Studio 54. They went on to tell me that Rubell and Schrager were the owners of Studio 54 and that they had recently been indicted for income tax fraud.

"Oh, I see . . . these guys are trying to plea bargain with the Justice Department. Trying to get off or have their sentence reduced by producing criminal information about me!" I would have taken the situation much more seriously if I had known then — as I would learn later — that Roy Cohn represented Rubell and Schrager, that he had taken the bogus charges to the Justice Department and had already leaked the story to the press.

But the agents told me nothing more, refused to comment on my observation and warned me not to try to talk with Jody until the FBI could interview him so that there would be no allegations of collusion between us.

It turned out that Jody was on a trip with the president down the Mississippi River. He called me the next morning after his interview.

"You weren't even with me the night I went to Studio 54," I told Jody indignantly. To me, the charges were utterly outrageous, lacked any credibility, and were obviously motivated by an attempted plea bargain. "Maybe this will be a three-day story and blow over," I suggested hopefully.

"Are you kidding?" Jody responded. "The president's

top aides, a president who is a born-again Christian, Studio 54, drugs . . . they will have to deal with it. Batten down the hatches because we are going to have a bumpy few days here."

But even Jody could not anticipate how seriously the charges would be treated. The next morning, the *New York Times* ran a headlined front-page story, which in turn stimulated calls to my office and the press office from the major networks and the top correspondents from other news organizations.

I sat in the office in the West Wing of the White House alone. Jody had been right . . . this charge against me was already a big story, and it was going to get bigger fast. I was totally vulnerable to these outrageous charges because they would be piled on top of all the other untrue but reported stories. I had very few real friends in the media who would stand up for me.

Still waiting for President Carter and Jody to return, I wrote the president a memo stating that I had not taken drugs and had never used drugs. I also said that I feared that my being under investigation while a member of his staff was unfair to him and I stated my intention to resign.

I was sitting in the Oval Office when the president and Jody returned. Jody was feisty, arguing that the charges were baseless and that most members of the press would believe us. I told him that I was not so sure after reading the *Times* story and seeing the flood of requests for interviews.

BEING PHOTOGRAPHED WITH JODY POWELL
BY RENOWNED PHOTOGRAPHER YOUSUF KARSH

Carter agreed with Jody but reminded us both that as the ultimate law enforcement officer of the United States, he would have to be careful and conservative in what he could say publicly.

After that conversation, I walked back into the president's small office, just off the Oval Office, handed him my resignation memo, and left.

In a few minutes, the president called me on the direct line and asked me to join him in the Oval Office. He came from around the desk, put his arm over my shoulder, and said, "Ham, your leaving will not help anything. . . . I will lose both ways. Some will see your resignation as confirmation of your guilt and I will be denied your services at a very critical time for the administration. It is in your interest and my interest to stay and fight this thing through."

The most damaging and outrageous treatment of the charges was a major story that led off the "CBS Evening News." It was introduced by Walter Cronkite, reported in detail by Mike Wallace, and finally concluded with an "analysis" by Bob Pierpoint, the White House correspondent. The three segments together lasted longer than eight minutes . . . almost half of the total "budget" (twenty minutes) of the entire news report.

The CBS News story focused on a trip I had made earlier in the year to a Democratic Party fundraiser in Southern California. Two well-known liberal fundraisers and political opponents of the Carter Administration (they were already actively raising funds for Ted Kennedy's primary challenge) told Mike Wallace that they had heard that I used drugs on that trip. Several other people who were interviewed also said that they had heard I had used cocaine, but they had not produced a single witness to my using cocaine.

I was devastated as I sat in my office and saw this outrageous report. . . . I felt like someone had punched me in the stomach. The Mike Wallace story took every single allegation and insinuation from the mouths of people I had never seen and did not know — however groundless or reckless — and treated them as absolute truth. Wallace accepted allegations made by third parties and discounted or rejected outright my unequivocal denial conveyed by Jody to the executive producer of CBS News, as well as the assertions by credible third parties that no one had ever known or even heard of my taking drugs.

Our denials were all for naught. Any reasonable person watching the "CBS Evening News" would have concluded that Carter's chief-of-staff was an out-of-control cocaine user and a jerk to boot.

After watching the CBS report, I began to think that my first instinct to resign was the right thing to do. Who knows, I thought, I might be asked to resign. I could not argue with anyone who went to the president (or came to me on his behalf) and simply said, "This thing is hurting the president . . . you need to step down."

It seemed that no one — not even the members of the press who knew me from covering the campaign — would risk coming to my defense or challenging the momentum of this story, which was running so strongly against me. It seemed to make no difference that my accusers were plea bargaining with the Justice Department and were represented by Roy Cohn. Had the press totally forgotten about the tactics he had honed in the McCarthy hearings?

The only person who spoke out on my behalf was Jimmy Breslin, a journalist whom I had never met but who had watched Roy Cohn and Company operate in New York City.

"Hamilton Jordan is the most maligned person in the nation today," Breslin wrote. "Whores shriek and deadbeats smirk that Jordan has sniffed cocaine in their presence. And the news industry rushes to make important their statements. The *New York Times*, using the claims of people from a place like Studio 54 . . . ran a story on the first page that left me with the impression that Jordan had killed several babies. CBS used six minutes of its evening news show to herald rumors spread by sleaze."

The investigation dragged on for ten months.

PRESUMED GUILTY

My grandfather used to say, "The road to hell is paved with good intentions."

I had become a victim of such good intentions — and had been practically to hell. With the abuses of the

Nixon White House and the "Saturday Night Massacre" (when Nixon had fired his own prosecutor, Archibald Cox) fresh in the national memory, we introduced a law that mandates the appointment of a special prosecutor when any serious charge is made against a "high government official." While the basic tenet of our legal system is that the accused is presumed innocent, under the special prosecutor's law — as a practical matter — we learned that the accused is considered guilty until he or she can prove their innocence.

The logic against me ran something like this: Jordan is guilty of outrageous social behavior . . . he made obscene gestures to the wife of the Egyptian ambassador, he has been a jerk around Washington, he was accused of taking a bribe from Robert Vesco, he probably has a drinking problem, so if he went to the "back room" at Studio 54, he probably used cocaine!

But truth ultimately prevailed, and I remember the "celebration" in my office in the White House on the afternoon that Independent Counsel Arthur Christy announced that the grand jury had voted 24–0 against bringing an indictment against me. Christy — who obviously had figured out the scam that Roy Cohn had almost pulled off — announced that there was no serious evidence against me and told a few key press people on background that I had been "set up" by Roy Cohn and friends.

Attorney General Ben Civiletti — who had replaced Griffin Bell when he resigned and had appointed the special prosecutor — visited the president in the Oval Office shortly before my public exoneration and told Carter that he had considered bringing indictments against Rubell, Schrager, and Cohn for their perjury and their obvious conspiracy to bring false charges against me. Attorney General Civiletti told the president that he had decided not to bring charges as it was "not in Hamilton's best interest to do so."

I wished the attorney general had asked me what I thought were in my best interests.

The spontaneous celebration that broke out in my West Wing office following the announcement that I had been cleared was awkward and embarrassing for me. Someone popped a bottle of champagne and friends from the White House dropped by or called to express their support. Some even "congratulated" me.

I was sure that I had not done anything to earn anyone's congratulations, and it was hard as hell to think that I had "won" anything.

I had embarrassed the president, and I had violated "Clifford's Law." Mr. Clark Clifford, a key aide to President Harry Truman and the dean of Washington "insiders," told me in my office soon after our inauguration, "Whenever the press is writing stories about the staff — good or bad — it is space that could have been devoted to the president and the administration's goals and policies."

To the extent that I cared about my "public reputation" — and at some level, I certainly did — I knew that it would be forever tainted by these silly allegations.

I should have taken some short-term satisfaction when Rubell and Schrager went to jail to serve time for tax fraud charges. However, after a brief stay in a minimum-security facility, they were out, celebrated in New York social and media circles.

Studio 54 finally closed as the disco era wound down, and Schrager and Rubell went on to other things. Rubell ultimately died of AIDS. Schrager opened the first of a series of trendy hotels in New York City and around the country and the world.

During the middle of the Studio 54 investigation of me, an anonymous person — maybe trying to be helpful or to even some old score with Roy Cohn — sent me some intimate photographs of Steve Rubell and Roy Cohn that insinuated a romantic relationship between the two. I did not know the real truth, but I did know that despite a highly publicized career of exposing people in government as "dangerous homosexuals" who were vulnerable to blackmail by the Russians, Cohn himself was widely believed to be gay.

I felt uncomfortable even looking at the pictures and never used them in any way. If the tables were turned, there is little doubt what Roy Cohn would have done.

And now, six years later, Roy Cohn was right here at the National Cancer Institute, fighting for his life just like the rest of us. And to think . . . he was right down the hall!

I remembered the scene from *The Godfather* where the assassin goes to the hospital to smother some ailing rat fink with a pillow. I relished the thought of walking into Roy Cohn's room, identifying myself, giving him a piece of my mind, and having him at least worry about my intentions.

Later that day, I used my friendship with a nurse to locate Roy Cohn's room. Ignoring the red "Warning" and "Posted" signs taped all over the door, I stuck my head in the door, ready to surprise Cohn and say my piece.

The room was dimly lit, and when my eyes finally focused, I could see that Cohn's famous bug-eyes were closed, his face and neck covered with dark splotches. The brash, in-your-face character from old news clips was taking loud and irregular breaths from an oxygen mask that covered his face.

I just stood there with my head poked inside the door for a few seconds, unable to enjoy his plight, seeing only another human being wasted by disease.

Suddenly I felt a tap on my shoulder. "Do you have a visitor's pass, sir?" the nurse asked.

Surprised, I mumbled an apology and hurried quickly down the hall.

Toward the end of his life, Roy Cohn's life began to catch up with him. A few months after I saw him at

NCI, the New York State Supreme Court, whom he denounced as "yo-yos" and a "bunch of blithering idiots," voted unanimously to disbar him from the practice of law, and said his behavior as a lawyer had been "unethical," "unprofessional," and, in one case, "particularly reprehensible."

Cohn did not take it laying down, showing people his personal "get well" notes from President and Nancy Reagan. He speculated in the *Washington Post* as to whether the president or first lady would attend his funeral and bragged about the fact that Attorney General William French Smith was a good friend and had attended both of his Reagan inauguration parties.

He died in August 1986. The *New York Times* repeated Cohn's claim that he had cancer. The White House issued a statement that "The Reagans are saddened at his passing and extend their sympathy to his family." Roy Cohn would have liked — and expected — that.

MAGIC WORDS

This part of my story ends where it began, with a doctor looking at X rays up against a viewing screen. The young NCI doctor held the films up to the light . . . one at a time.

"Nothing there, nothing there, nothing there . . ."

DUNCAN DOBIE

BALD AND BLOATED AFTER CHEMOTHERAPY

When he paused at one film, I held my breath.

"Nope, that's just scar tissue. Mr. Jordan, based on these X rays, I am happy to tell you that you are a CR for sure!"

"CR" stood for "complete remission" and meant that blood work, X rays, and palpation had revealed no sign of cancer. It didn't mean that there were not some hidden cells beyond the view of these modern tests and instruments.

"There is not a sign of cancer anywhere."

I gave the surprised doctor a bear hug that caused him to drop the X rays all over the floor. I babbled a quick apology, left him down on his knees picking up the film, and started running down the hall to the pay phone. I heard him yell down the hall after me, "Now, you will still have to have regular checkups and be followed closely. . . ."

"I understand, Doctor. I understand. Thanks so much!" I yelled.

By the time Dorothy answered the phone, I was sobbing like a baby.

We had probably beaten cancer. It had not been easy. I was completely bald, bloated from steroids, and vain enough that I stopped shaving in the bathroom so I wouldn't have to look at myself in the mirror. The industrial-strength chemo with the "kicker" tacked on at the end had taken its toll on my body, and, according to my doctors, had rendered me sterile.

The good news was that my cancer was gone. There were no guarantees. I would live under a cloud for a few years with monthly checkups, X rays, and blood tests. But I had earned at least the chance to live a normal life with Dorothy and watch my son grow up.

I considered myself a very lucky man.

ALBANY, GEORGIA

I followed my doctors' orders closely and continued to be checked regularly . . . once a month, then every three months, then six months, and finally once a year.

I didn't become a hypochondriac, but I listened to my body more closely than most and didn't hesitate to visit a doctor when I had a real pain or worry. I also began to see a lot of stories in the press about skin cancers and decided to see a dermatologist in 1991.

As I was shown to the exam room, several pale young doctors in their white coats dashed from room to room. No tans here, I thought.

Dermatologists must be the busiest, fastest-moving docs anywhere. Like so many in medicine, they are being squeezed financially, and their only way to stay even is to increase their volume of patients.

"These are the barnacles of age, Mr. Jordan," the young doctor said as he went over my body, covered only by boxer shorts. He would occasionally pause to peer through the magnifying gizmo strapped to his head at some suspicious mole or wart.

He moved quickly over my legs and arms, then came to an abrupt stop on my lower arm, asked for a can of spray that freeze-dried and numbed the spot, flicked it off with a small knife and then mumbled something into a hand-carried recorder clipped to his white jacket.

"This one is probably going to need to be biopsied. Did you get a lot of sun exposure when you were young . . . sit out in the sun a lot?"

"Only for about ten years, doc," I said. "I was a lifeguard every summer from junior high through college."

"Did you wear sunscreen?"

"In 1960 . . . are you kidding? We used Johnson's Baby Oil with iodine in it. Wasn't that as good as sunscreen?"

He laughed out loud, "Probably about the worst thing you could use. That iodine didn't block the ultra-violent rays, and that oil just baked your skin instead of protecting it."

"It sure made me tan."

"And probably produced these couple of spots which are probably some kind of skin cancer."

I quit joking when I heard the dreaded "c" word and turned into Dr. Jordan. "Skin cancer? If you looked at my chart, you know I've had my share of cancer. Do any of these moles look cancerous?"

"Won't know until the pathology comes back," he said matter-of-factly. "But I wouldn't worry. None of these is of any size or consequence."

Yeah, I thought. No consequence to you.

Again, I had to think about cancer.

It was disturbing to me that something I had done thirty years before might be expressing itself today in some kind of abnormal cell growth.

I thought back to those hot summer days at the Elk's Club where I was a lifeguard, teaching the children of doctors and lawyers to swim as little tots, then baby-sitting them at the pool year after year while their dads played golf and their moms tanned themselves around the pool, sipping Cokes through the day and piña coladas — topped with little paper umbrellas — in the late afternoon.

By the end of the summer, I would be so brown that my father used to joke that folks were going to think I was integrating the Elks' Club pool. . . .

It was already hot enough that summer of 1961, but the temperature went up all over town when the civil rights struggle came to Albany.

A normally sleepy town tucked away in deep southwest Georgia, Albany was the retail hub for our agricultural corner of the state. The pace quickened on

Saturdays as pickup trucks and cars from all over South Georgia swarmed into town, filled with farm families, the men dressed in overalls or brown khaki work clothes and the women in loose-fitting cotton dresses. Some were plain looking .· . . others had on their "Sunday best." They had come to "Aw-benny" with their paychecks and shopping lists.

This was the summer that Dr. William Anderson, an idealistic black physician, organized "The Albany Movement" to test the new Supreme Court ruling that required the integration of all public facilities. The organization's actions were aimed specifically at eliminating the "White Only" signs at bathrooms and water fountains, the most powerful symbol of legal segregation throughout the South, and to give black Georgians access to the local bus system and trains.

But the good intentions of Dr. Anderson were not enough. While Anderson had energized the black community, he had no plan for translating their activism into leverage with the white authorities. After several months of public marches followed by arrests, trials, and releases, there would be more marches, arrests, and trials. The word on the street was that the "movement" was floundering, losing steam, and having trouble finding fresh marchers as many "locals" could not afford more time in jail or fines.

In addition, there was starting to be competition between locals and outsiders for "leadership" of the Albany Movement. The leadership of SNCC — the

Student Nonviolent Coordinating Committee — which had sent key national leaders into Albany, was increasingly concerned that other civil rights organizations might be invited in.

While the movement dominated the headlines and gripped the local community, nothing was really happening: there was no dialogue with the public officials and no strategy. The white community, in the meantime, smugly "stiffed" Anderson, refusing even to talk to him or his lieutenants. By strictly enforcing the law and never resorting to highly publicized violence (as Chief Bull Connor would later commit in Birmingham), the white establishment made its strategy obvious: they simply planned to wear the Albany Movement down.

Flustered and uncertain as to how to play his hand, Dr. Anderson finally turned to his old Morehouse classmate, Martin Luther King Jr., and asked him to come to Albany for a speech. King — who was still developing the nonviolent tactics that would later prove so successful — accepted the invitation for a single appearance simply as a favor for an old friend.

However, once King arrived in Albany and made a powerful and moving speech at Mt. Shiloh Baptist Church, he immediately realized that he had invested his personal reputation in the Albany Movement. What had been a local and state story became a major national story overnight.

At the age of seventeen, I saw Dr. King's first march

in Albany. Despite pleas in the *Albany Herald* for its white readers to refrain from glorifying these "trouble-makers and outside agitators," my father surprised me by inviting me to go downtown with him one Saturday morning for Dr. King's first march. In a few minutes, we found ourselves standing in the middle of the all-white crowd, two or three deep along both sides of Pine Avenue, the main street that was lined with huge palm trees.

By now it was December, and the day was cold and overcast. An eerie silence pervaded the downtown area as most stores and offices had closed and the major streets were roped off.

After several months of public demonstrations, a ritual had developed among the marchers and the police. The marchers would gather at one of the large black churches for coffee and donuts, speaking and singing and seeking inspiration from one of the gifted preachers from around the South who would recruit the worshipers to join in the march. They would then pour into the street in a flood of black faces, accentu-ated by the occasional priest or nun in official garb, and would march a scheduled route to the front of City Hall, where the police would stop them and ask them to disband. They would politely refuse and would be arrested, always without incident.

But with Dr. King in town, all bets were off. Rumors were everywhere that card-carrying communists, armed with weapons, were pouring into town. The

KKK responded by calling for a rally in Albany and declared an "alert," asking its chapters to send "white militia" to Albany prepared to fight.

We couldn't see the marchers yet, but we could see the advance guard of policemen on motorcycles that preceded them. Necks strained and people stood on tiptoes. We began to hear a quiet noise that became a chorus as it got closer and closer. Finally, we could make out the words.

> "We shall overco-o-o-m-me
> We shall overco-o-o-m-m-m-me
> We shall overcome some day."

The marchers rounded the corner and came into full view as they filled Pine Avenue. I was surprised — most of the marchers were high school and college age with a sprinkling of kids who were barely teenagers. It was easy to pick out the familiar face of Dr. King with his dark overcoat on in the front line, marching in locked arms with other men who looked like clergy.

Particularly noticeable was a toffee-colored, handsome young man marching next to King who looked like he was in high school. I would learn later that he was a preacher from Thomasville, Georgia . . . Reverend Andrew Young.

Someone else in the crowd had noticed the light-skinned marcher as well and shouted, "Go home, you high-yellow nigger!"

A farmer in overalls standing nearby voiced the ultimate fear, "That's what happens when you integrate . . .
niggers will marry our daughters!"

"Over my dead body!" another retorted.

"Go home, Commies!"

"Get a job, you lazy niggers!"

"Two, four, six, eight . . . we ain't gonna integrate!" a
group of teenagers repeated time and again.

The group kept marching down Pine Avenue. "My
God," my father muttered as he held up his hand and
pointed, "There's Hattie!"

Sure enough, bringing up the rear were several rows of
black women in their Sunday best, and right in the middle was our housekeeper of over fifteen years, Hattie
Jackson. In her sixties, Hattie was a proud, quiet women.

What did this mean . . . "our" Hattie in a protest march?

The crowd moved at a quick pace on down Pine
Avenue until they reached the area of City Hall where
they were met by a phalanx of big policemen in riot
gear, tall black boots, white helmets, and black leather
jackets. They chatted nervously among themselves,
standing across the street about five feet apart, twirling
their billy clubs.

Positioned in the middle to "receive" the leadership of
the Albany Movement was Chief Laurie Pritchett, a
large, round-faced man, who had won the grudging
respect of the black leaders by "shooting straight" with
them and never allowing for violence or mistreatment
of the prisoners.

THE ALBANY MOVEMENT: DR. MARTIN LUTHER KING JR.,
DR. WILLIAM ANDERSON, AND POLICE CHIEF LAURIE PRITCHETT

Looking down at the top of King's head, the chief blared over his bullhorn, "You are violating the laws of our city by marching without a permit. You have two minutes to disperse . . . you have two minutes to disperse or you will be arrested!"

There was no response from the crowd. Dr. King and another marcher knelt in prayer. After a minute, the light-skinned young man pulled out a bullhorn and stuck it in front of Dr. King. Avoiding the chief's glance, Dr. King said in a strong, clear voice, "We are exercising our constitutional rights to peacefully assemble. We are marching today to protest the failure of the City of Albany to allow its Negro citizens and taxpayers the use of its public facilities. We have broken no law and seek no trouble. We only request that you enforce the law of the land, Chief Pritchett, and allow us to exercise our rights."

There was no reply, and the chief looked around nervously as a television camera crew pressed through the crowd with a microphone extended to try to pick up the exchange. Chief Pritchett studied his watch . . . waiting for the two minutes to expire. It was going according to plan. The marchers knew they would be stopped, the Chief knew that they would not disperse, and the group expected to be herded into the area between City Hall and the jail where they would be led one-by-one up the stairs to be booked and put in jail.

The protest marchers waited quietly for what seemed like eternity. Most stared straight ahead at Chief Pritchett.

The Chief finally looked up, pulled out his bullhorn, and said calmly, "You have refused to obey my orders, and you will now be arrested. Do not resist arrest, and you will not be harmed."

The large crowd moved quietly into the area between the city jail and the courthouse, which were connected by a large, brick building, thus surrounding the group on three sides. The policemen took their billy clubs and gently prodded and poked until all the demonstrators had squeezed into the small space. They had started to sing again, but you could hear the voices of some starting to talk or complain out loud . . . one or two of the children began to cry.

I was never sure what happened next . . . whether the demonstrators had stumbled and tripped or had been pushed to the ground by a nervous or overzealous cop, but people began to pile up in the narrow alley and several ear-piercing screams penetrated the winter air.

A couple of the onlookers laughed, and one yelled out, "Looks like a bunch of niggers in a sardine can!"

Several marchers locked arms and circled King to protect him. Soon, the entire crowd had dropped to the ground, the singing had stopped completely, and screams and cries echoed out of the enclosed area.

The white onlookers began to shout their approval.

I looked anxiously for Hattie but could not find her in the sea of black faces. It turned out that a young lady had fainted and was being passed above the crowd to the outside where some medics were soon attending her.

My father, a normally gregarious man, had watched in silence, then tugged at my arm and said, "Let's go!"

I was gripped by the spectacle in front of me and just stood there until I felt another hard tug. "Listen to me, Hamilton, we are leaving," he said sternly, "Right now, do you hear me?"

He was silent for a while as we drove home. Then he started talking. "Those people ought to be ashamed of themselves . . . getting those children into that mess. I'll be glad when they all leave town."

"What about Hattie?" I asked.

"Hattie better be careful, or she's going to be looking for work somewhere else."

My father harbored no sympathy for the protesters and repeated the argument that the good, local "colored folks" had been brainwashed by these "outside agitators." But my father was a gentle man who would never harm another human being. I could tell that he was uncomfortable with what we had seen that day . . . the ugly mood of the crowd, the raw hate that we could almost feel.

In reading about the protesters in the local papers, I had felt threatened. These people were out to destroy our way of life. But seeing it up close was entirely different, and witnessing the march that afternoon changed my thinking forever. For the first time, I felt real shame in my life, watching quietly while decent people and children — including our own dear Hattie — were herded into the alley just like animals.

Later, I would mark that day as a moment of moral failure in my life. I had an opportunity to take a stand, to risk something . . . instead, I had just stood there. Like so many other "decent" white Southerners, I kept my outrage and my shame to myself.

We worried that Hattie might be in jail. When she did not answer her phone, I begged my father to call the jail and check on her.

"This is none of our business, Hamilton. Hattie got herself into this mess, and I am not going to interfere. If she calls and needs bail, I will help her, but I am not going to stick my nose in this civil rights business!"

We were surprised the next Monday morning when Hattie, who regularly rode the six o'clock bus across town to be at our house by seven, slipped quietly into the house, wearing her crisp white "maid's" uniform. She even gave me a good-morning hug, which was something she used to do every day, but less often now that I was a teenager. Later, I would wonder if that hug was a way of forgiving all of us and Hattie's way of bringing Dr. King's message into our home: I love you even though you have mistreated me and my people. That hug stuck with me the rest of the day.

Hattie followed her usual routine: took the garbage out, cleared off the breakfast dishes, and assumed her usual place at the sink to do the dishes before she went room to room, making up the beds and gathering clothes to be washed and ironed.

My father appeared in the kitchen dressed in a dark

suit, ready to go to work. He looked surprised to find Hattie there, and I wondered what he would say . . . or if he would take her aside and scold her for getting involved in the march.

"Good morning, Hattie," he said.

"Good morning, Mr. Jordan."

"Nice day, isn't it?"

"Sho is, Mr. Jordan, sho is."

I realized then that my father was confused by all that was happening and felt the same shame as I did.

No one in our family ever said anything to Hattie about her "marching," and she never mentioned it to us. She did seem to be spending more time at "church activities," which was a clear signal to us that she was heavily involved in the Albany Movement.

It was through Hattie's quiet commitment that I began to appreciate the depth of the civil rights struggle. I was sure that all over the South there were "good colored folks" playing the same game as Hattie . . . working in the homes, restaurants, garages, and businesses of white people for meager wages, but slowly and surely putting aside their fears and becoming the foot soldiers of the movement.

A few years later, Hattie surprised my mother when she announced that she was taking the day off so that she could drive people to the polls to vote in the 1964 presidential election. It was as close as she ever came to publicly acknowledging her political activism.

The courtroom was packed, but we knew some ladies in the clerk's office who slipped us into a row in the back just as the judge called the court to order. One section of people were scribbling furiously on pads, and we figured out they were the national press.

Judge Abner Israel presided. I knew him well—he was one of my father's golfing partners in his regular Sunday game. The judge peered over his glasses, glaring first at the press, then at the group of blacks huddled around a table in front of the courtroom. I half stood, hoping to see Martin Luther King, but could not find him.

Judge Israel tapped his gavel a couple of times softly, and the blacks standing around the table quickly took their seats. Several of the men in the press area were turned around in their seats, talking to one another until Judge Israel firmly banged his gavel.

"In the event some of you have not had the occasion to appear in this Court," he drawled, "I will expect order and respect." Unable to hide the sarcasm in his voice, the judge forced a slight smile and looked at the area where the press was sitting, "To our friends in the press who may not be accustomed to Southern courtesies, you are welcome here, but the very same rules apply. No talking, no noise. Clerk, read the charges."

A wiry little man, wearing a black suit, white shirt, and red bow tie, stood up and read the charges, "City of Albany versus M. L. King. Dr. Anderson and others . . . For organizing a march without permit, refusal to obey an officer's order, and disturbing the peace."

"Defendants," Judge Israel snapped. "Stand up."

As the famous head of Martin Luther King Jr. popped up, my brother leaned over and whispered, "He looks like Mighty Mouse."

I thought at first that he was trying to be funny, but when I looked at King, I knew what he meant. The small head perched on top of the compact body featured large ears and a slim mustache. King wore a tapered, dark suit that fit him snugly. He looked quite dapper.

"Mr. King, Dr. Anderson, you have heard the clerk read these charges against you . . . how do you plea?"

"Not guilty, your Honor," King said first in a rich, clear voice. The others joined in.

"Alright," the judge said. "Proceed."

The prosecutor slowly lifted his large, pear-shaped frame and waddled toward the Judge. "The City of Awbenny, Jawga, calls Chief of Police Pritchett."

The red-headed police chief took the stand and recounted how Dr. King had led a march that was not authorized, had disrupted traffic and commerce in the downtown area, and had refused his requests that the marchers disperse. After several minutes of questioning, the prosecutor turned to the judge and said, "Your Honor, the City rests."

The Judge turned in the direction of Dr. King and the others, "The defense will now be heard."

An elegantly dressed black attorney rose and started to speak, and I remember thinking that this was the first time that I had ever heard a black man talk like a white person. "My name is Donald L. Hollowell. I am an attorney for the NAACP, and am licensed to practice in New York State, Washington, D.C., and Georgia. Assisting me is the Honorable C. B. King of Albany and Miss Constance Baker Motely of New York State."

C. B. King and the other black attorneys rose briefly, acknowledged the judge, who just glared, and sat back down.

"I know C. B. King," the judge said sarcastically, seeming to enjoy the fact that he had withheld the simple courtesy of a "Mister." "I do not know these other lawyers and do not know if they are properly licensed and able to appear before this Court."

Hollowell jumped to his feet: "With respect, your Honor, these are distinguished attorneys," and started to rattle off the credentials of his fellow counsels.

"I don't care what you know about these others, Mr. Hollowell. You have not made the proper arrangements for these people to practice in my Court, and they will not be allowed to speak here today."

"But your Honor," Hollowell protested, "I would like to bring to your attention that this team has practiced before the Supreme Court, participated in the landmark *Brown vs. Board of Education* suit. . . ."

Abner Israel held up his hand, "Enough, Mr. Hollowell, enough . . . Please do not waste the Court's time. I do not need biographies here . . . proceed."

Hollowell went back to the table where King was sitting with the other black lawyers, picked up a handful of paper, turned around, and held up a document. "Your Honor, if it pleases the Court, I would like to read some selected portions of the United States' Constitution. Starting with the Fourteenth Amendment, which states . . . "

Bam, bam, bam . . . Israel was red in the face as he banged his gavel over and over and over again. I thought he might just explode.

"Mi-s-s-s-t-e-r-r Hol-l-o-w-e-l-l," he dragged the name out sarcastically. "I do not need instruction from you or anyone else on the U.S. Constitution. Do you understand?"

"In all due respect, Judge Israel," Hollowell quickly countered, "The Constitution of the United States is THE ultimate authority. The city's refusal to permit Dr. King, Dr. Anderson, and the members of the Albany Movement to peacefully assemble is a violation of the Constitutional rights under Article . . . "

Judge Israel was now standing, . . . "Stop, Mr. Hollowell, stop . . . you will not make speeches to me in my court about the law."

"Your Honor, my client has the right to a reasonable defense. Is this Court not aware of the following Supreme Court cases," and Hollowell started reading cases in a loud voice while the judge — his face beet red — was banging his gavel nonstop.

Hollowell continued to read in a normal voice.

"Mr. Hollowell, cease, Mr. Hollowell, stop right now!"

It looked like Judge Israel was not only losing his temper but losing control . . . the hearing was not going the way it was supposed to. The judge quickly ordered a recess, got up, and started toward his chambers.

Mr. Hollowell droned on.

The judge stopped at the door, turned, and glared at Hollowell and warned loudly, "One more word, Mr. Hollowell . . . one more word and you will find yourself in contempt of this court and spending the night in jail."

This time Hollowell stopped. Israel flashed a satisfied smile until he heard another voice.

"Judge Israel, please hear me out," a deep voice boomed.

A hush settled over the courtroom, and the judge turned to see Martin Luther King Jr. standing erect, his hands outstretched as if asking for quiet.

"Judge Israel, neither I nor my attorneys mean any disrespect to you personally or to this court. But this is a court of law. How can our very own Constitution and the rulings of our highest court be of no interest to you or no relevance to this court? Can you answer that question for me, Your Honor? Do you recognize and accept the rulings of the U.S. Supreme Court?"

The Judge froze at the door, his eyes no longer were filled with hate . . . he seemed confused as to how to deal with King's direct and respectful appeal.

King's deep voice rang out again, "Please answer me, Judge, do you recognize the U.S. Constitution and the rulings of the U.S. Supreme Court?"

The judge slammed the door and escaped to his chamber as the court crowd turned noisy with reporters trying to yell questions to King and Anderson, huddled at their table, surrounded by their legal team.

It was learned later that Judge Israel had met in his chambers with some of the city fathers who told him in no uncertain terms that he was losing control and that the routine hearing could turn into a "circus," giving Martin Luther King Jr. a platform for making derogatory speeches about Albany.

Using Police Chief Pritchett as an intermediary, the city fathers began a negotiation with King, Anderson, and their team with the main objective of getting King out of town in hopes of taking the wind out of the Albany Movement.

Judge Israel returned and — in a calm voice — refused to hear any more witnesses and postponed the trial of King and the others for sixty days.

The jail full of protesters were released, and King suddenly found himself on the courthouse steps, having to defend and rationalize the "deal" struck between the city fathers and his representatives. King claimed victory, and later told a cheering crowd at Mt. Shiloh Baptist Church that those in jail had been freed and that a biracial commission would be set up to address the overall issue of desegregation. King also mentioned that his presence in Albany was no longer needed.

Even as he spoke, Chief Pritchett was denying that the city had agreed to any "deal."

The press was hard on King, calling the "deal" between the city and King "a stunning defeat" for King's reputation.

King returned to Albany in July 1962 to be sentenced for his previous December marches. Faced with the choice of paying a $178 fine or serving forty-five days in jail, King took the jail sentence, fully expecting a long and publicized stay in jail to give the Albany Movement new life and momentum.

Two days after he began to serve his sentence, he was released and told that an anonymous, well-dressed black man had paid his fine. King was flustered and complained that, "For the first time, I was sorry to be out of jail."

It turned out that through local publisher and Democratic Party Chairman James Gray, the city fathers had been in direct negotiations with the Kennedy Administration, hoping to defuse the growing tensions. Federal Judge Robert Elliott, a Kennedy appointee, issued an injunction that ordered King not to violate the local ordinances. This meant that King would have to violate a federal order if he marched again. King felt uncomfortable disobeying a federal order (and possibly offending the Kennedy brothers) so he watched from the sidelines as the Albany Movement took to the streets. After Judge Elliott's injunction had been overturned by an appeals court, King returned to the streets and to jail.

After starting his third jail sentence, local Judge Durden suspended King's sentence and conceded that the Supreme Court had overruled the local segregation ordinances. Even Albany Mayor Asa Kelly admitted that Dr. King had " . . . accomplished his objectives."

King and the leadership of the Albany Movement celebrated their victory as "the end of segregation in Albany, Georgia." They found it quite hollow, however, when young Negroes — trying to integrate the public library, pool, and other facilities — simply found them all closed.

King returned to Albany, led marches, and received suspended sentences. The white leaders seemed to always find a way to give King a short-term victory and then take it away through the shrewd use of the media, the local laws, and the nonviolent tactics of Chief Pritchett.

King always regarded the Albany Movement as one of the early and most important lessons of the civil rights movement. The local black leadership thought that King's presence itself would assure success and alleviate growing strains between the local and national civil rights leaders. Instead, King's presence only sharpened these tensions over leadership and tactics.

The regular marches in Albany continued for a while, became smaller in size until they became only occasional gestures, covered only as a local story as King moved on to Selma, Montgomery, Chicago, Washington, and finally Memphis.

Change came hard to the South . . . and to the Jordan family. My father could never bring himself to say "Negro" properly, but he stopped saying "nigger" around us and usually used the word "colored" or "nigra," which was the "polite" compromise between "nigger" and "Negro."

In the late 1960s, the reality of integration hit close to home.

A proud veteran of World War II, my father was serving as chairman of the local draft board, a thankless volunteer job that he treated very seriously. With the Vietnam War raging, the Johnson Administration was pushing hard for these local boards — which exercised considerable authority over the fate of young men of draft age — to add black members in symbolic recognition of the increasing number of black draftees and volunteers.

After much discussion, the board invited Dr. Thomas Jenkins, the tall, dynamic president of Albany State College (the local Negro teachers' college) to serve on the Board. Jenkins, a shrewd and gregarious leader, knew how far to push for what he wanted without permanently alienating the white elites. He made quick friends with the white members of the draft board and quickly became a force in their deliberations. It was not long before my father was telling us that Tom Jenkins was a "good man" and a "good example for the colored race."

However, my father was more shocked than touched when Dr. and Mrs. Jenkins, unannounced, dropped off a pecan pie at our home for the Christmas holidays.

Hattie seemed to take special delight when she walked into the family room where my father was reading the afternoon paper to announce, "Mr. Jordan, Dr. and Mrs. Thomas Jenkins are at the *front* door."

My father — flabbergasted to have a black couple at our front door paying a social visit — maintained enough composure to exchange pleasantries and to invite them in. He seemed surprised that they accepted his invitation and were soon sitting in our living room. He offered them a drink, and before long they were sipping on bourbon-and-water and making small talk.

Later, laughing at his predicament, my father said, "I suppose if I had invited them to spend the night, they would have slept over."

The Jenkins' visit was a landmark in my father's life. Although he told people about it in a joking way (I always thought to preempt or dispel any notion around town that he had actually invited them for a social visit), I could tell that he had taken a perverse pride that the proud black educator had chosen our home to visit.

Years later, when Dr. Jenkins was appointed by Governor Jimmy Carter to be the first black person to serve on the State Pardon and Paroles Board, Tom Jenkins invited my father to attend his swearing-in ceremony in Atlanta. My mother was sick and unable to go, but Hattie heard them talking about the trip and asked my father if she could ride up with him as Dr. Jenkins was one of her "personal heroes."

While my father didn't want to have to bother with

Hattie, neither did he have the heart to turn her down. So my father — with Hattie riding in the back seat, which was where blacks always rode when in a white person's car — drove all the way to Atlanta. My mother made sandwiches for them to eat in the car so my father would not have to deal with the complicated issue of the two of them eating at a public facility. My mother could not resist kidding my father later that, as they drove away, it looked like a black woman had a white chauffeur. He did not find her observation amusing.

My father reported that he learned more about Hattie in that drive than he had learned in fifteen previous years. Trapped in the car for six hours, they talked about things never mentioned before, and it changed their relationship forever.

I doubt if my father ever thought about the irony and contradictions of that trip to Atlanta: my father in the front seat and Hattie — part-time maid, part-time civil rights worker — in the back, driving to Atlanta to see his friend, the first black man appointed to an important state board (and the first black to ever come to our *front* door for a social visit) sworn in.

My father was very proud of Dr. Jenkins's success and loved to tell friends that Jenkins's service on the draft board had demonstrated his effectiveness in his dealings with whites and had been a major factor in his appointment to the important statewide position.

Years later, I made the trip home to Albany to attend Hattie's funeral at the church where she had sung in the choir for forty years. I was the only white person there.

My mother and father stayed home. They loved Hattie and appreciated her years of loyal service. But they simply could not bring themselves to attend a black church. What would people say if they heard that they had gone to black funeral?

THE CANCER GENE

Four years had passed since my bout with lymphoma when I got word that my mother was back in the hospital. Dorothy and I canceled our after-Christmas vacation with our young son and our three-month-old baby daughter. I drove all night to my mother's hometown in South Georgia to be with her.

Although she was finally coming to the end of her long battle with lung cancer, my mother had thrown — in the words of my sister — a "hissy fit" when she heard we had canceled our trip.

She struggled to sit straight up in the hospital bed and finally got vertical enough to shake her finger as she scolded me: "I will not stand for you canceling this vacation with Dorothy and those precious children. I'll jump out of that window over there if you try to stay here with me instead of taking your family on this trip. I am just fine in this wonderful hospital, and your sister is going to stay and keep me company."

I wasn't particularly worried about her jumping out the window since her room was on the ground floor, but I had no doubt that my dear mother would make my "visit" with her just miserable if I did not bend to her will.

It was this same indomitable spirit that had helped to keep her cancer at bay now for more than five years in spite of the dire medical predictions.

I remembered clearly the young doctor showing us the spot on the X ray indicating that the cancer had come back on her remaining lung only months after the removal of her other lobe. He was the same young doctor who, at her original diagnosis, asked my mother if she smoked.

When my mother responded that she did not smoke, my sister's jaw dropped.

"Have you ever smoked, Mrs. Jordan?"

"Yes, I did."

"For how long?"

"About fifty years."

"How much?"

"Four or five packs a day."

"When did you stop, Mrs. Jordan?"

"Yesterday, Doctor . . . right after you told me I had lung cancer!"

When my mother's cancer recurred, the young doctor had described her new challenge and prognosis: "As we feared, our initial strategy of removing the one cancerous lobe was not successful. The cancer has now spread to the remaining lung, and there is a significant amount of disease in that lobe. Radiation to that tumor will probably reduce the size of the tumor or stop its growth, but it will not get rid of it and will reduce her lung capacity even further. Since she has multiple sclerosis on top of her cancer, this only complicates her ability to breathe normally and comfortably. Bottom line is that I don't want to make her a respiratory cripple by overdoing the radiation."

The doctor told us that he would radiate her "tactically" to fight the cancer when it interfered with her quality of life, but that sooner or later, it was going to hit a spot or a vital organ where there was nothing else left to do.

"Doctor," I said, "someone has to ask, how long is she likely to live?"

"Your mother is one tough lady, but the cancer plus the MS . . . I hope that I can help her to have another pleasant six to nine months, maybe a year, but it will be downhill after that, very difficult for her, and she will not last long."

That was over five years ago, and here my mother was still bossing us all around, playing bridge every Wednesday with her "girl friends" and absolutely immersed in the lives of her seven grandchildren, with their pictures, little notes, and Christmas and birthday cards taped all over her refrigerator, her dresser, and the walls of the family room.

It seemed that my choices were pretty clear . . . go on our vacation or stay here with my mother and catch hell nonstop from her for not going. As I hugged her goodbye, she pulled back, looked me in the eye and said, "You understand, don't you, son, I am damned tired of being sick!"

"Mama," I said, smiling as I hugged her, "I know what you mean. . . . I know what you mean!"

It bothered me after I left the hospital and had time to reflect on it . . . my mother's "one cancer patient to another" tone of voice, saying she was "tired of being sick." It was as close as she had ever come to complaining about her cancer or even suggesting that cancer might prevail.

But her spirit was otherwise strong and my hunch was that it was just a low moment, being put in the hospital right after a wonderful Christmas with our family. We were all going to have to get used to her being in and out of hospitals for the next few months and then try to get used to life without this special woman who had loomed so large in all of our lives.

Twenty-four hours later, Dorothy, the kids, and I were out riding in a horse-drawn carriage in the beautiful foothills of West Virginia, covered by a sprinkling of light snow, when I suddenly turned to Dorothy and — for reasons I could not explain then or now — simply said, "My mother just died."

Dorothy was startled at my strange declaration and we rushed back to our hotel room to call her. The message light on our phone was blinking, and I was not surprised when I listened to my sister's voice asking that I call her immediately at the hospital. When she answered, I could tell that she was fighting tears as she told me that our mother had "passed away" peacefully that morning without any pain or discomfort. "I think she was just tired of fighting and not feeling good and finally just threw in the towel."

After the funeral, we invited all of her close friends, neighbors, and family members from out of town to come by our family home to visit. Not surprisingly, we easily fell into telling funny stories about my mother's rich and wonderful life. As the afternoon wore on, local family friends had come and gone, and we were left to take comfort in the company of my mother's and father's remaining brothers and sisters and their children.

As I looked around the room, I was struck by how many of my aunts and uncles shared a common experience with my mother and father and me.

My father's brother had prostate cancer. My mother's brother had prostate cancer and her sister was battling breast cancer.

I mentioned this to Uncle Frank, eighty-five years old, a wrinkled and gentle plain-spoken peach farmer from Talbotton, Georgia, who was actually my father's cousin.

"Hamilton," he said, "seems like we just got the cancer jinx in the Jordan family."

"On both sides," Uncle Hamilton, my mother's brother, added. "Our mother had two different cancers in her lifetime and Daddy had prostate cancer. What about Clarence? Did Clarence Jordan die of cancer?"

"No, no, no," Uncle Frank said, shaking his head vigorously, "My little brother Clarence didn't die of cancer. . . . Clarence died of a broken heart."

True, Clarence did not battle cancer, but he fought all of his life against something as deadly and pervasive as cancer — the prejudice and hatred that were so deeply ingrained in the world he grew up in.

UNCLE CLARENCE

My father's family lost everything in the stock market crash of 1929 and the Great Depression, and his father died shortly afterwards of a heart attack. Overnight my Daddy went from being the son of one of the wealthiest men in middle Georgia to selling Maxwell House coffee door-to-door to support his family. He spent more and more time with his first cousins who lived nearby in Talbotton, a small farm town in middle Georgia known as the "peach capital" of the world.

His seven Talbotton cousins became more like siblings. The middle son was named Clarence.

When I was growing up, Clarence Jordan was a

mysterious figure in the life of our extended family, rarely present at family reunions or the annual gatherings in Talbotton for Thanksgiving and Christmas when we would choose up sides and play football on the big lawn speckled with pecan trees before stuffing ourselves with turkey, country yams, and pecan pie.

I can remember family members whispering among themselves about "what Clarence was doing" and shaking their heads with disgust.

When I was eight or nine, I remember saying to Uncle Clarence on one of those rare occasions when we did see him, "We see Uncle Frank and Uncle George and Uncle Robert all the time. We never see you except at weddings and funerals."

The big man squatted down to look me right in the eye, smiled and hugged me, then pulled back: "Well, Hamilton," Clarence said, "You are half right . . . you only see me at family funerals because you have to be invited to weddings," he laughed with a twinkle in his eyes. "I love your daddy and mamma so much that we have got to get together more."

But we didn't, and Clarence continued to be the "black sheep" in the family. It was a long time before I would understand.

Later on, when I was in high school, Clarence, Florence, and their children visited us every couple of weeks throughout one summer. They always came at night unannounced, piled out of the same old beat-up car and usually brought pecans or peaches from their farm in a brown paper bag. They wore overalls or khaki pants, obviously farming clothes, but as we romped and played in the backyard, the kids seemed pretty normal to me. What didn't seem normal, though, was that as soon as Clarence and Florence left, my parents would shake their heads and agree that it was "just a shame what Clarence was putting his family through."

As I later came to understand, by this time (the late 1950s) Clarence Jordan was a marked man. Clarence himself eventually explained to me the reason for his frequent visits to my family that summer. Martin Luther King Jr. and "The Albany Movement" were trying to integrate the public facilities, and over a three- or four-month period, King and the leadership of the civil rights movement were in my hometown, either in jail or in hiding in the houses of supporters. Clarence told us that he saw Martin — as he called him — regularly during this period and that on the way out of town, he and Florence had enjoyed dropping by our house at night to catch up with the "Albany Jordans."

As I grew older, I learned to both understand and appreciate my unusual Uncle Clarence and began to visit him — without my parents' knowledge — once or twice a year, starting with my junior year in high school.

G. K. Chesterton once said, "The only problem with Christianity is that no one has ever tried it." Chesterton obviously never met my Uncle Clarence.

In 1942, while Martin Luther King Jr. was in the seventh grade, Clarence Jordan founded an interracial commune in rural South Georgia. It was eleven years before the Supreme Court declared the "separate but equal" doctrine unconstitutional and more than two decades before blacks could drink from a public water fountain or use a public bathroom. Strict segregation was not only prevalent in the South . . . it was legal.

Clarence Jordan committed himself to living his faith — ironically the same Baptist faith that rationalized segregation and racism, the same faith that first tried to silence him, then tried to run him off and finally attempted to destroy him.

Clarence lived his life in "scorn of the consequences," and risked everything . . . the love of his parents, siblings and friends, and the lives of his own wife and children. For twenty-five years, Clarence and his family stood alone against the rising tide of the white South's worst violence and bigotry.

Asked by a reporter after one bombing if he were ever scared, Clarence responded, "Was I ever scared? I am always scared, particularly for my wife and children. But being scared is not the question . . . the question we face every day is whether or not we will be obedient to a system and to a group of people who insist that we hate and mistreat our fellow man."

Martin Luther King Jr. called him "my friend, my mentor, and my inspiration." Recalling their first meeting, Dr. King said, "When I first invited him to speak at Dexter Street Baptist Church (in the early 1950s), Clarence told us about his interracial commune in rural South Georgia. It was shocking and inspiring . . . and sounded too good to be true. Here was a son of the old South, a white Baptist preacher doing what we were just talking about doing. I went to Koinonia later to see it for myself and couldn't wait to leave because I was sure the Klan would show up and kill us both."

Corranzo Morgan, a black farmer, recalled, "I almost fell off my chair when Mr. Jordan came over the first time, shook my hand, and invited me and my family for Sunday dinner. I hemmed and hawed and finally said we wuz busy. I'm athinking, this young white boy must not know that coloreds and whites eating together jest isn't done . . . he is going to get his-self kilt. My next thought was that we might get ourselves kilt too . . . living cross the road from him."

"When we first heard about Clarence Jordan and Koinonia," Andy Young recalled, "we considered it too radical, too dangerous. Martin and I were trying to get folks the right to ride on the bus and to shop where they wanted . . . huge challenges back then. But here Clarence was — smack dab in the middle of Ku Klux Klan country — going for the whole loaf. Clarence did not spend all his time telling others what to do or making a fuss about it . . . he just kept living his faith. And

Clarence put all the rest of us to shame until we did something about it."

Clarence himself was a bundle of contradictions. He was, in the words of his biographer, Dallas Lee, "a gentle man who thundered against injustice, a nonviolent man who stared down the Klan, a genuinely humble man who could walk into the home of a rich man and say, 'Nice piece of plunder you got here.' He was a dirt-farming aristocrat, a good ol' Georgia country boy with a doctor's degree, a teacher with manure on his boots, a scholar in working clothes."

Clarence's faith was not a remote, prissy, sanitized doctrine or ritual but a gritty, folksy, in-your-face way of life, based on respect and love for all of humanity and applied to every decision and every action. The hard moral choices that Clarence forced on a defiant white South were often sugar-coated in his rich sense of humor and sounded a bit less threatening when delivered in his melodious drawl.

The civil rights struggle dominated every aspect of Southern life in the 1950s and 1960s. Clarence saved his special scorn for his own Baptist Church. The white churches generally and the white Baptist churches specifically, caught in this moral cross-fire, were the major force for rationalizing segregation and maintaining the status quo.

"Here you are," he lectured a group of Baptist ministers, "sitting smugly on your hands while the greatest moral dilemma since the Civil War is ravaging your communities. What is your response, ye moral pillars of the South?" Clarence mocked: "I'm sorry, but I can't afford to get involved."

"Brother Clarence," one minister protested, "you are being too hard on us . . . every person here is praying for you."

"Save your prayers for each other," Clarence thundered. "You need them more than we do. Your silence in the face of this hate and violence makes you an active accomplice to the cowards who shoot up our homes, beat our children, and bomb our farms."

No one clapped as he sat down.

TALBOTTON, GEORGIA

Clarence Jordan was born in 1910 in the central Georgia town of Talbotton, where his family were prosperous farmers and merchants. The middle of seven children, there was little in his early years to suggest the remarkable life he would lead.

The fires that would erupt later in his life simmered quietly for years as young Clarence began to measure and weigh what people said against what they did. He attended Sunday School at the First Baptist Church and learned to sing the same songs of love and faith sung by Baptist children everywhere. One of his favorites went,

"Red and yellow, black and white,

They are precious in His sight,
Jesus loves the little children of the world."

Years later, Clarence would write about the torment
this little ditty caused him:

It bothered me greatly . . . even as a
child. Were the little black children
precious in God's sight just like the
little white children? The song said
they were. Then why were they
always so ragged, so dirty and hun-
gry? Did God have favorite children?
I was puzzled and started to think
that maybe it wasn't God's doings, but
man's. God didn't turn these black
children away from our churches —
we did. God didn't pay them low
wages — we did. God didn't make
them live in another section of town
in miserable huts and pick rotten
oranges and fruit out of the garbage
for food — we did. Maybe they were
precious in God's sight, but were they
in ours? My environment told me
that they were not very precious in
anybody's sight. A nigger was a nigger and must be kept in his place —
the place of servitude and inferiority.

The sprawling Jordan home was just down the street from the courthouse. Clarence recalled that the jail was about one hundred yards from his home and a group of "chain gang" convicts was often camped in the jailhouse yard. Fascinated by these strange characters so different from his own experience, Clarence began passing through the camp in the afternoons after school. The acquaintances he developed gave him a glimpse of life that was totally alien to what he was being taught at home and in church:

> I saw men with short chains locked between their feet to keep them from running, men bolted into the agonizing shame of primitive pillories, men beaten with whips or their bodies torn under the stress of the "stretcher" — a small frame structure in which a man could be placed with his feet fastened at the floor and his hand tied to ropes above him that extended to a block and tackle on the outside. I saw that almost all these men were black. This made a tremendous, traumatic impression on me.

Another indelible boyhood memory was of a revival one summer night, when Clarence from his place in the church choir looked out into the congregation and saw the warden of the chain gang get carried away as he sang "Love Lifted Me." But the next night he was awakened by agonizing screams of one of his chain gang friends; the warden had the man on the stretcher. "I was torn to pieces," recalled Clarence. "I identified totally with that man in the stretcher. His agony was my agony. I really got mad with God. If the warden was an example of God's love, I didn't want anything to do with Him."

Clarence carried the contradictions of his early life with him to the University of Georgia where he studied agriculture but continued to read his Bible. The summer after graduation, he went to ROTC camp to complete the training that would allow him to be commissioned an officer in the U.S. Army. It was while playing soldier atop a galloping horse that what mattered most to Clarence became abundantly clear. Later, he wrote about it:

> The class that day was a mounted drill held on the edge of the woods. I was on horseback and galloping through the woods with my pistol and saber drawn. We were to shoot the cardboard dummies and stick the straw dummies with our sabers. Every time I would shoot one of those dummies, that verse, 'But I say unto you, love your enemies,' would flash through my mind. . . . At that

moment, I saw the conflict between
the mind of Jesus and the mind of the
commanding officer. It was crystal
clear that Jesus was going one way
and I was going another. Yet, I
claimed to be his follower.

When Clarence had completed the obstacle course
and cleared the woods, he found his commanding officer, dismounted, and resigned his Army commission on
the spot. The officer tried to talk Clarence out of such a
rash decision. When he got nowhere, he suggested that
Clarence should become a chaplain.

"I told him," Clarence said, "that would be the worst
thing I could do. I could not encourage someone else to
do something that I myself would not do."

His course was set, and he surprised family and
friends when he announced that he had decided to
become a preacher.

THE SOUTHERN BAPTIST SEMINARY, LOUISVILLE

His fellow students at the Southern Baptist Seminary in
Louisville were not sure what to make of the tall, high-
hipped, slow-talking Georgia boy who quickly earned
the nickname "Tall-Bottom." Clarence soon began
preaching and working in the poor black neighborhoods
of the city, and the idealism of theology school crashed

headlong into the harsh reality of the urban poor. Clarence became a familiar face in the crowded shanties of "South Town," befriending people and inviting black families to dinner at his modest apartment on campus.

For these activities, needless to say, Clarence was rebuked by some of his professors. He offered a spirited defense, using the very Bible teachings of those now chastising him to devastate their objections. The flustered head of the seminary finally ended the discussion: "Brother Jordan, you are supposed to minister to these unfortunate people, not entertain them in your home. It just is not done."

Outraged to find the same hypocrisy in theology school that he had found as a little boy at the Baptist Church in Talbotton, Clarence set a course from which he would never depart: "I made up my mind then and there that I was going to try to live my faith . . . not act it."

Clarence was inspired to a new vision by Florence Kruger, the tall, blue-eyed daughter of German immigrants who worked as the assistant librarian at the school. Clarence started spending more and more time at the library with Florence, talking about their beliefs and faith, and soon they announced they were to be married. They conceived a plan to return to the rural South to establish a "demonstration" project where they could "live their faith" and combine their religious beliefs with their practical knowledge of agriculture to help the rural poor, black and white.

KOINONIA — THE EARLY YEARS

In July 1942, Clarence and Florence Jordan and Baptist missionaries Mabel and Martin England opened their "demonstration project" in rural South Georgia near Americus, down the road from Plains. They called it Koinonia, the Greek word for "community."

Clarence had a strategy for realizing his dream. He wrote one of his friends from theology school:

> At first, we'll set up simply as farmers, trying to win the confidence of the people as good citizens and good neighbors. Once we feel that we are part of the community, we will try to bring in some of the principles that we believe in. In this way it will be growth from within instead of a system imposed from without. We'll hold all things in common, distribute to people according to their need, and every worker will be given an equal voice in governing our community.

Fifty years later, it is difficult to comprehend the courage of white people in rural Georgia establishing an interracial commune flying under a Christian banner. Indeed, Clarence's vision was so radical for the times that it was not initially understood or taken seriously by

CLARENCE JORDAN AT KOINONIA

either the local whites or blacks. The white churches found the young man fresh out of the seminary a witty and entertaining preacher. Later, Clarence would say, "They must notta listened to what I was saying."

But the tolerant atmosphere changed when the good folks of Americus began to see blacks and whites eating, living, and working together at Koinonia. It was doubly threatening that Clarence was one of their own . . . a Georgia boy, a Baptist, and a farmer. Twenty years later when "outside agitators" were swarming into the South in support of Dr. King's activities, a familiar refrain of the white Southerner was, "You just don't understand the South." They could never say that about Clarence Jordan.

The churches led the attack when they realized that "race-mixing" was part of the Koinonia agenda. The local Baptist church voted Clarence and the Koinonians out for "violating the social customs of our community." Clarence feigned surprise: "I don't understand your action in throwing us out. If we are sinners as you suggest, we are in bad need of being at church and getting straightened out. If we are the saints, you are in bad need of our fellowship."

THE DIFFICULT YEARS, 1955-1965

When the Supreme Court ruled in 1953 that the "separate but equal" doctrine was unconstitutional as applied to public education, the South prepared to refight the

Civil War. Yet here, in the heart of Dixie, was Koinonia, which embodied the worst fears of the white South. The people of Sumter County resolved to either drive them out or snuff them out.

It started out as a series of mean-spirited "pranks" — threatening phone calls in the middle of the night, the signs torn down at the roadside stand on Highway 19 to Atlanta where Koinonia sold its eggs and farm products to passers-by, sugar poured into the gas tanks of cars and trucks parked at the farm. As the Koinonians tolerated these minor annoyances with little complaint, the harsh jokes turned into a stream of violence.

In July 1956, a bomb was thrown into the roadside stand in the middle of the night, causing significant damage.

Koinonia responded by running ads in the local paper, stating clearly that they were not there to harm anyone and asking the same of their "neighbors."

The plea not only fell on deaf ears but earned the official condemnation of the Sumter County district attorney: "Maybe what we need right now," he said, "is for the right kind of Klan to start up again and to use the buggy whip on some of these race mixers. . . . I had rather see my little boy dead than sit beside a nigra in the public schools."

With this official sanction, the violence escalated and became more focused on Clarence and his family. His son, Jim, subjected to constant abuse at the local high school, was shipped off to finish high school among friends in North Dakota.

Still, in the face of mounting violence, Clarence always argued against abandoning their project, saying that if they left, it would only give encouragement to the forces of hate and evil. As Florence expressed it at one meeting, "There was never any feeling in Clarence's mind or my own that we should leave. We would not be the first Christians to die for their beliefs and we certainly would not be the last."

One night while Florence and Clarence were driving from Americus to Koinonia, a pick-up truck of good old boys started to pass them, slowed down long enough to yell insults at them, then darted ahead. When Clarence rounded the curve, the same pick-up truck was blocking the road, and three men were standing in the middle with shotguns. Clarence screeched to a halt and later claimed to have set a "world record for a 180-degree turn on a dirt road. I recalled that the Scripture said, 'If a man strikes you on your right cheek, turn to him both heels.' They may have shot at us, but I didn't hear it if they did because I was traveling faster than the speed of sound."

Reports of violence against them was routinely reported to the police and routinely dismissed. In January, their roadside store was bombed again . . . this time completely destroyed, with a loss of more than seven thousand dollars' worth of goods.

The violence moved closer to home. In the middle of the night on January 27, 1957, the peace of Koinonia was interrupted by screams as a machine gun strafed several houses, miraculously missing the inhabitants. Several days later, two cars rode by the farm in the early evening and fired shotguns at the lighted playground where the children were playing volleyball. As the children ran for cover, Clarence erupted with anger and ran toward the cars shaking his fist and yelling, "Come back here and face me, you cowards! Come back!"

As the intensity of the violence directed at Koinonia increased, Clarence searched for ways to protect his followers. In 1957, he wrote to President Eisenhower:

> Dear Mr. President,
> A peaceful community of sixty men, women, and children is facing annihilation unless someone in authority does something about it before it is too late. Groups of ten to twelve cars are harassing us every night. We have been bombed, burned out, and shot at. Our children are beaten going to and from school. Until the Supreme Court decision and the rise of the White Citizens' Council, we were not molested. Since then, our life has become difficult and our existence precarious. We have been told that the end is near, but we shall not run, for this is America. Should freedom perish from our land,

we would prefer to be dead. Someone
in authority must do something before
it is too late.

Eisenhower did. He passed Clarence's letter on to J.
Edgar Hoover, who promptly initiated a federal investi-
gation of Koinonia as "known race mixers and probable
Communists." Hoover also passed the letter on to the
Georgia Attorney General and encouraged the Georgia
authorities to begin their own probe.

Emboldened by the federal and state actions —
ironically instigated by Clarence's plea for help to the
president — the Sumter County grand jury launched
its own investigation with the goal of ridding itself of
Clarence Jordan and Koinonia once and for all.
Clarence was called to testify and told a reporter when
leaving the courthouse, "I tried to explain to the good
folks on the grand jury the difference between Karl
Marx and Jesus Christ . . . ended up they didn't know
very much about either one of 'em."

The grand jury issued a public report which held the
white community blameless and accused Koinonia of
"bombing itself" and creating "incidents" for the purpose
of drawing attention and "stirring racial passions."

When Clarence read the report, he said that the
white community had sanctioned the past crimes committed against them and had given a "hunting license"
to anyone who wanted to do them harm.

BOYCOTT

Having tried and failed logic and violence, the white community turned to coercion and imposed a highly effective boycott on Koinonia. It was simple — any people caught selling anything to Koinonia would themselves be boycotted. It applied to everything — gas, fertilizer, food, and medicines — and soon the Koinonians were traveling seventy-five to one hundred miles to get outside of the area of the boycott and to make anonymous purchases in cash.

When the Birdsey Feed Store in Americus (owned by a Macon man who knew Clarence's parents) refused to honor the boycott and continued to sell to Koinonia, his store was completely destroyed by a bomb. The good people of Americus meant business.

During the boycott, a prominent Americus banker wrote Clarence's father, who was on his deathbed, to tell him that "Your integrationist son is tearing our Christian community apart." The sick old man sent for his son and chastised him for "bringing shame on our good Christian name." For once, Clarence bit his lip and did not argue. Instead, he marched into the banker's office unannounced, jerked the surprised man up by his necktie, and promised him, "The next time you bother my sick daddy, I am going to forget about Jesus Christ for about fifteen minutes and beat the hell out of you."

1965-1969 . . . HARD TIMES

By the late 1960s, Koinonia was running out of steam. The hard work of the civil rights struggle had moved to the ballot box and the courtroom. While people came and went, the actual number of devoted Koinonians dwindled sharply. Some left because of the violence, others left simply because it was a hard and demanding existence.

Clarence began to spend more and more of his time preaching and writing, translating the Bible into a modern version cast in contemporary times. He called it the "Cotton Patch Version" (which Harry Chapin turned into a successful off-Broadway musical in the early 1980s).

Unlike Clarence, I kept my own doubts about "the system" to myself but still managed to cultivate our friendship. The last time that I saw Clarence, I had just returned from Vietnam and was going to work for his neighbor, Jimmy Carter, who lived just a few miles down the road and was going to run for governor of Georgia. I wondered what Clarence thought of him.

"He is a nice fella, Hamilton, but he is just a politician."

He was in a reflective mood that day as we sat in his "writing shack," a cozy ten-by-twelve-foot structure where Clarence read, wrote, and studied. I had not seen him in two years, so there was some catching up to do. He talked with a touch of sadness about the past, the defection of so many of their people from Koinonia, and the hatred that persisted. I was surprised to find him low.

"Haven't you accomplished a lot here?" I asked.

"That is not for me to say. I hope that we have made a good try at living according to the Lord's teachings."

Then he continued: "We have made progress, but not much." And holding up his large, rough hands, he put his thumb and forefinger almost together. "Every inch, every centimeter has been so hard . . . and at such a great price. But we have survived and persevered. We have survived," he repeated. "A tiny light in a sea of hate."

He looked out the window of the little shack as if counting the years and remembering all the people who had come and gone, all the violence directed against them. His eyes glistened. He continued, softly, "We have accomplished so much less than we had hoped for when we bought this old run-down piece of land. I underestimated the raw hatred of these people for their fellow human beings . . . the lengths to which they would go to justify their own corrupt system . . . the good people who lacked the moral courage to speak out. My greatest disappointment was the hypocrisy of the church . . . these so-called preachers who should have been pillars of strength and examples, moving people toward understanding and reconciliation. Instead, they were moral cripples whose silence aided and abetted those who hate us and try to destroy us."

Clarence told me that he would never leave Koinonia, but that their struggle for economic justice must move to the cities, where the urban poor had no jobs, no houses, and no hope. He called his new vision "Dream for Humanity," which was focused on the reality that people without a home were not a family, could not live in dignity, and did not have self-respect. "I think the Lord is pushing me to be practical in my old age," he chuckled, "and become a house-builder in the city instead of a farmer."

Six months later, Clarence suffered a massive heart attack while working in his writing shack. His son Lenny gave him mouth-to-mouth resuscitation but was unable to revive him. Panicked calls went out to the emergency room and several doctors . . . but no doctor would risk coming to Koinonia, particularly not to save Clarence Jordan's life. Clarence was dead at age fifty-nine.

The "good people of Americus" tried to humiliate Clarence in death as they had been unable to do in life. The coroner refused to come to Koinonia to issue a death certificate and insisted that the body be brought to him. Millard Fuller, one of Clarence's most devoted disciples, loaded Clarence's limp body into the back of a broken-down station wagon and drove him to the hospital, where he had to wait before bringing Clarence in. The coroner insisted on doing an autopsy. Millard called Florence at the farm for approval; she assented, and in a few hours Fuller was ready to carry Clarence home.

"They may have cut out his heart," observed Clarence's older brother, Frank, when he heard about the autopsy. "But they couldn't get his soul."

Remembering Clarence's opinion of funerals ("a waste of money on an empty shell . . . you can send a kid to college for a year on what some people spend celebrating their dead selves"), Millard Fuller put a few coins, a pocketknife and a Timex watch — representing all of Clarence's worldly possessions — in a paper bag. On the way back to Koinonia, he found a used shipping crate and strapped it to the top of the car. The next morning, following a simple service attended by about a hundred friends, Clarence, with his few possessions, was buried in his work clothes in the pine box in an unmarked grave.

I was in Savannah organizing for Jimmy Carter's campaign for governor when my mother called me to tell me Clarence had died. I immediately asked about the funeral arrangements, but I was already too late.

I felt sad not to be able to say goodbye to this great man whom I had barely known but who had brushed against my own life. I smiled when I thought about Clarence's sudden exit . . . he left this earth just as he had lived — on his own terms as defined by his God.

No one would be more disappointed than Clarence that the hard lessons of his life and faith would still be so highly relevant twenty-five years later. It would bring tears to his eyes to realize that, forty years later, some of the grandchildren of the white Southerners who bombed Koinonia, shot up his home, and beat his children still today occasionally burn black churches in the South.

On the other hand, it would bring a smile to his face to know that one of his followers — Millard Fuller — took his new vision and transformed it into Habitat for Humanity. Clarence would also find it a great and pleasant irony that his farmer-politician neighbor down the road, Jimmy Carter, was one of its main supporters.

Maybe this good man who demanded so much of himself and others would take some small satisfaction from all of the good that had come from the example — he would call it "witness" — of his own life. But I doubt it.

PATHOLOGY REPORT

It took several days to get the pathology report on the "samples" that the dermatologist had nipped from different areas of my arms and face.

When I heard a message on my answering service from my doctor, I knew that it meant trouble. . . . My experience is that the nurse calls with the good news and the doctor calls with the bad.

"Mr. Jordan, it is a good thing that we took those samples because one showed an early skin cancer which we need to take care of."

Cancer number two was a hell of a lot easier than

cancer number one . . . a skilled dermatologist numbed the area around the cancerous lesions, quickly excised them — with a generous margin — and sewed me up with a few stitches.

And it was over . . . I hoped.

ON THE BEACH

August 1995. We were on our annual family vacation on the Outer Banks of North Carolina. It was a glorious morning, the warm sun bearing down from a cloudless sky while a steady breeze blew the sea oats back and forth on the dunes separating the wooden houses — built high on stilts — from the beach. I was standing on the back porch of our house watching my three children (conceived naturally, despite dire medical predictions) through binoculars as they romped in the surf with more than a dozen of their Pennsylvania cousins. In the old days, people might tease me that my kids look like the mailman . . . the 1990s version would be that these surprise children looked like the FedEx man. However remarkable their conception,

Hamilton Jr., Kathleen, and Alex on the beach

Dorothy and I considered ourselves especially blessed to have a wonderful daughter and a second son.

Hamilton Jr., eleven, was riding his "boogie board" in the morning surf while his little brother Alex, three, puttered around looking for shells. I could barely see Kathleen's laughing face who, at age six, was being "buried alive" by several cousins who were scurrying around and covering every inch of her little body with handfuls of wet, white sand.

Dorothy and her two older sisters had lined up their beach chairs in the usual spot on the edge of the surf so they could watch the kids while they baked in the sun, read their paperbacks and talked, pausing now and then to splash their feet in the water or to get up and call to a couple of the older boys who were out a bit too far on their surfboards.

I tried to enjoy the view but could not help myself as I paced back and forth on the wooden deck, anxiously awaiting a call from my doctor.

It had started earlier that week during my annual physical exam. Among other things, I had a digital rectal exam of my prostate, which was normal, and also had a simple and relatively new blood test called PSA (for prostate-specific antigen), useful in detecting prostate cancer.

A day after my exam, the nurse called to give me my report: "Everything looks good." I asked specifically about the PSA as it had edged up slightly the last couple of exams. "Your PSA is 3.9 . . . within the normal range."

While I understood it was technically "normal," I also knew that it had shot up a full point since my last check-up. I had read a Mayo Clinic study that indicated a rise of more than .75 in a year was considered abnormal. Mayo had also developed an "age-adjusted PSA" that meant my "normal" PSA was actually slightly elevated for a man my age. Armed with this new information and acutely aware of my own cancer history, I was not about to sit back and relax.

My regular doctor — Dr. Bill Waters III, who is one of the greatest doctors anywhere — was on summer vacation, so I called Dr. Paul Hatcher, a respected urologist in Knoxville who had been my urologist when we lived there. I described my situation and asked him if I should have an ultrasound, which would allow him to "look" at the prostate gland. He agreed and got my undivided attention when he told me that one out of three men with an elevated PSA have prostate cancer.

He did the ultrasound the next day but found no suspicious spots. "As long as we are in here with the ultrasound, we could do a random needle biopsy which will sample your prostate . . . it's the only way to know for sure if something is going on."

That was no decision. I knew first-hand the advantages of being aggressive in screening as well as in treating cancer and urged him to proceed.

"We are being aggressive," Hatcher admitted, "but you'll know where you stand." Using a "needle gun," he took six samples of my prostate, each of which would be examined under the microscope overnight. The procedure was only mildly uncomfortable.

I gave the doctor my vacation number and arrived back at our beach house just in time to join the Scrabble game, an after-dinner ritual that divides the family into fiercely competitive teams. I was glad to lose myself in letters and words and hoped that I seemed normal to Dorothy. We played into the night, and I was relieved when Dorothy called it quits and went to bed.

Our game ended after midnight, and I sat out on the porch with Dorothy's two older sisters, our feet propped up on the railing as we were swallowed up in a perfect summer evening: a full moon, teenagers huddled around small fires up and down the beach, and the sound of the surf crashing against the sand. It was the next-to-the-last night of our vacation.

"I am expecting some bad news tomorrow," I announced, "and I thought it would be better for you both to know while we are all still together so you can help Doffy (the family nickname for Dorothy, their baby sister)." I told them about my biopsy and shared my worst fears. They sat and listened quietly, reaching out to touch me and finally hugging me as they tried to reassure me.

Susan thought that I was unduly worried because of my first cancer. "Everything will be okay."

"Whoever heard of anyone your age having three different cancers?" Nancy asked.

Lying in bed that night, I tried to rationalize my situation, counting stats instead of sheep . . . going over and over again the same facts. Dr. Hatcher had found no "suspicious areas" with the ultrasound. Only one out of three men with elevated PSAs has prostate cancer. And Nancy was right. What are the odds of a person having three different cancers by the age of fifty? I calculated it must be one in one hundred thousand.

But these mental gymnastics provided little comfort. Despite the seemingly favorable odds, I had a strong premonition that I had another battle to fight with cancer.

I didn't sleep well, got up early, made a cup of coffee, and sat on the porch watching the sun come up while I waited for the call from my doctor on my prostate biopsy. By the time that sun goes down, I thought, I would either be facing cancer again or laughing about my overreaction to a silly blood test.

Dorothy called from the bedroom, and when I walked in, she was sitting straight up in the bed. "Hamilton, what's going on? Something's wrong!"

I had not fooled her after all. I hated to tell Dorothy that I might have cancer again. Although she would think me foolish for this thought, I felt like I had failed her.

"Dorothy, I am afraid that I have prostate cancer."

Later, she would tell me that she heard me say the words but simply could not absorb them. "You what?" she said in a disbelieving voice. "You have what?"

I told her my story of the rising PSA and my needle biopsy the day before. She was visibly relieved. "You don't have cancer, Hamilton, you are worried that you might, but you don't know for sure." Like her sisters, her hunch was that I had overreacted.

She was right, but, at another level, I knew that she respected my instincts and feared my premonition. She pulled me onto the bed, gave me a big hug, and said, "No matter what happens, we have a guardian angel looking over us."

The phone rang around ten.

"Mr. Jordan, this is Dr. Hatcher. . . . Sorry, but I do not have any good news for you. Your pathology is back and you do have prostate cancer."

I was really not surprised and heard myself asking, "What is my Gleason?" The Gleason score is a number assigned by the pathologist from the analysis of prostate cancer cells under a microscope. A low Gleason (3 or 4) is a slow-growing cancer that often requires no treatment in older men while a high Gleason (8 or 9) means the tumor is aggressive, fast-growing, and more likely to have escaped the prostate gland.

"Your Gleason is a six . . . in the middle. In a man your age a Gleason 6 prostate cancer has to be treated." He told me I needed a CAT scan and a bone scan to see if there was any evidence of cancer spread outside of my prostate. My own father had died of prostate cancer, and I remembered his doctor telling us, "The horse is out of the barn." Now, twenty years later, would I get the same death sentence?

I made plans to leave that night to return to Knoxville to have my tests. During that afternoon on the beach with Dorothy and my kids, I found plenty of excuses for extra hugs. As I watched my children, I wondered if they would grow up without a father. How many more beach vacations would we enjoy together?

While facing my first cancer, I did research on childhood memories and learned that children under the ages of three to four have only the vaguest memories of lost parents. By the age of six or seven, children have some specific memories, and children over ten have full and rich memories. I could not stand the thought that my younger children might not even remember me. I started thinking about making a series of video tapes that might capture who I was and would express to them my special feelings for each one of them. Could I pull that off?

As I often do, I put Kathleen and Alex to bed that night. I laid between them on the double bed, made up silly stories and ended with our usual "Five Finger Prayer," which little Alex proudly led, bowing his head, folding his chubby hands together, and raising his little fingers one at a time: "Thank you, God . . . I love you, God . . . I am sorry, God . . . help others, God . . . help me, God . . . Amen."

Totally relaxed and in a state of pure joy, I watched them drift off to sleep. It was tough to break the spell, get up, say goodbye to Dorothy and Hamilton, drive to the airport in a hard rain, and start to think once again about cancer.

My tests in Knoxville the next morning were routine . . . drinking a gigantic, twenty-ounce cup of dye — poorly disguised as "orange juice" — before the bone scan and the CAT scan. As always, the hardest part was the waiting, and wondering what the technicians in the other room were saying as they saw my film. Was it — "This poor fellow is in bad trouble!" or "This guy has dodged a bullet!"?

I pumped them for clues. You can sometimes squeeze good news out of nurses and technicians — a wink or an "I'm sure you'll be okay" — but they always, always let the doctor deliver the bad news. I struck out with this crowd; they told me absolutely nothing. It worried me. As I hand-carried the film over to Dr. Hatcher's office, I pulled out a couple of the X rays and held them up to the light. I couldn't see a damn thing but that didn't make me feel much better.

Waiting for doctors to read your X rays must be like waiting for the jury foreman in a capital punishment trial to read your verdict. Someone you hardly know is about to tell you whether you are going to live or die. All it takes is a little spot on an X ray that was not there before to indicate that you have cancer. With my follow-up checkups, I have been through this ordeal dozens of times — it never gets easier.

Dr. Hatcher was matter-of-fact as he examined the films one by one: "There is no evidence on the bone scan or CAT scan that your cancer has escaped the prostate. This means that we have probably, and I stress probably, caught it early."

I breathed — literally — an audible sigh of relief. Calmly, he outlined my options:

- radiating my prostate over a period of time in hopes of killing all of the cancer cells;
- implanting radioactive pellets in my prostate, which would have the same effect; or,
- removing my prostate through surgery.

Hatcher explained that many patients considered the radiation options the "easy" choices as they avoided the surgery and some of its possible complications. Yet, he pointed out, there was no long-term evidence — over ten years — that radiation or implants were as effective as surgery. In fact, most urologists currently believe that surgery provides the best long-term cure rates.

"Doctor, with three young kids, I need a home run . . . tell me more about the surgery."

"The operation to remove the prostate is major surgery. But the good news is that IF the cancer is confined to the prostate, once the prostate is removed, you are cured. Short-term, you'll have some incontinence problems as a result of the surgery . . . long term, you should have none. There is a significant risk of impotency, which is greatest in older men but much less in men your age."

He continued. "It is not only major surgery . . . it is also delicate surgery where a millimeter can mean the difference in success or failure." Dr. Hatcher encouraged me to take my time in making my decision and advised that if surgery was my choice, I should select a surgeon who had done at least a hundred of these operations and who currently performed at least fifty a year. "I will only operate on you after you have considered all your options as well as other surgeons." He gave me a short list of the best prostate surgeons in the country. In an age when many doctors fight to hang onto surgical patients, Dr. Hatcher was unconcerned and confident in his own skills and knowledge. I had great confidence in his integrity and in his ability.

I had missed my flight back to Atlanta but was anxious to get home as Dorothy and the kids were driving in from the beach. I was determined to be waiting for them in the driveway to share my good news.

I rented a red convertible with a tape player, bought a handful of "Golden Oldies," grabbed a Big Mac and fries, and hit I-75 South. I put the top down, turned up the volume, and sang at the top of my lungs all the way to Atlanta. I got some strange looks from others who saw a middle-aged geezer in a flashy convertible, driving a bit too fast and singing "Sugar pie, honey bunch . . . You know that I lo-o-o-o-ve you, I can't help myself . . ." They probably thought I'd just won the lottery . . . and I had. I woke up that morning thinking that I might die. While there were no guarantees, I knew now that I might live — that was something to celebrate!

DECIDING WHAT TO DO

The day after my return from Knoxville, I got a call from Jimmy Carter. I assumed it was about some activity at the Carter Center as those of us who know and care for him understand that President Carter is not given to idle chit-chat.

"Hamilton, I haven't seen you in a while, but you have been on my mind a lot the last two or three days. I have been worrying about you."

I was flabbergasted to hear that he had been "worrying" about me at the very same time I had been on my medical roller coaster. Outside of my immediate family, no one knew about my diagnosis.

"Mr. President, I have been worried about myself. . . . I have just found out that I have prostate cancer."

"Oh no, Hamilton," he said. "I'm so sorry to hear that."

I thought about his own family's sad cancer history, the fact that his father and three of his four siblings had died of pancreatic cancer at a young age. Jimmy Carter was the only one left.

"You really didn't know about my situation?" I asked the president.

He convinced me his phone call was spontaneous. He said that he would be praying for me and asked for a report after my surgery.

"Mr. President, based on this call, you'll know my outcome before I do!"

While touched by his kindness, I was stirred even more by the mystery of his call. I had not spoken with President Carter in several months . . . how had he sensed that something was wrong with me? Coincidence, divine intervention, whatever . . . I was happy to have Rosalynn and Jimmy Carter in my corner.

Back at home, I began my research to determine if surgery was the best option and, if so, where to have that surgery. For the next several days, I was either on my phone or on the Internet in my home office. I called a number of medical institutions, talked with fifteen or twenty doctors and researchers, ordered books and tapes, and had printouts of medical studies from on-line services scattered all over the floor. Dorothy started calling me "Dr. Jordan."

The choices became increasingly clear. For a relatively young man like myself with a medium-grade cancer that we hoped was confined, the choices were surgery or some form of radiation. While the studies that contrasted surgery versus radiation yielded comparable results for the first five to ten years, there was growing evidence that the surgery provides a better long-term cure rate.

After immersing myself in the subject, I became convinced that a lot of men who should have prostate surgery avoid it due to a general fear of the operation and the highly publicized risks of impotence and incontinence —

which are seldom explained or quantified and sometimes exaggerated. When I weighed my enormous obligations to my family against the possibility of a little physical inconvenience or some compromise in my own personal pleasure, there was really no decision to make. It was more important to be alive and to have at least the possibility of a long life with my wife and children.

As I told Dorothy, "I can't have sex if I am dead!"

The top name Dr. Hatcher had given me was Dr. Patrick Walsh, head of urology at Johns Hopkins. I was already aware of his international reputation; in fact, he had treated my friend Dick Riley — former governor of South Carolina and Secretary of Education in the Clinton Administration — who had been diagnosed with prostate cancer. (Dr. Walsh successfully removed his prostate, and Dick is enjoying good health today.)

Dr. Walsh had not only built a great urology program (rated number-one in recent years by *U.S. News & World Report*), he had pioneered a new surgical procedure that improved cure rates while preserving the nerves which control continence and potency. I located a tape of Walsh performing his surgery and watched it alone late one night.

I was all the more absorbed upon learning that the patient was a man my age with young children. Dr. Walsh, a slight figure in surgical garb, mask, and glasses, narrated as he worked: "I am making a midline incision," as his knife sliced quickly through the man's abdomen from the navel to the pubic area as if it were jelly. My pulse quickened. I wondered if I should watch this, but I was quickly riveted.

Walsh's movements were precise and sure, as he separated the muscles and then cut through the dorsal vein, tying it off and creating the "bloodless field." This was one of the critical features of the procedure that Walsh had developed, allowing the surgeon to see clearly the prostate gland, the nerve bundles, and the surrounding area.

The atmosphere in the operating room was business-like. The only sounds were the occasional clink of instruments, the sucking sounds as an assistant struggled to keep the key areas dry with the suction, and Walsh's crisp directions: "Clamp, please . . . sponge stick, please . . . sharp right angle, please."

He paused occasionally to "teach," pointing out the rectum, the bladder neck, the urethra, and the nerve bundles that ran along the sides of the prostate.

Next, he cut through the urethra, then "eyeballed" the wafer-thin nerve bundles that run along the prostate. In this case, they appeared not to be affected by the cancer, and after a series of snips, he gently lifted both nerve bundles off the prostate gland itself. He then separated the prostate from the bladder neck, removing the gland. He then rebuilt the urinary tract, sewing the urethra directly to the bladder, installing the catheter and some temporary drainage tubes. After inspecting his work, he began to sew the man up.

After "closing," he pulled off his mask and cap, revealing kind eyes and a boyish face, and talked with passion about "his patients" and prostate cancer. Pat Walsh was a man on a mission: to defeat prostate cancer.

As I turned the VCR off, I realized for the first time that I had a layman's understanding of the prostate and the surgery to remove it. Pat Walsh was not only a great surgeon; he was a first-class teacher.

I went to bed 100 percent convinced that the "radical retropubic prostatectomy," created and performed by Dr. Patrick Walsh, was my best bet for being cured.

DR. PATRICK WALSH AND JOHNS HOPKINS MEDICAL CENTER

I made the first trip to Johns Hopkins alone in early August.

It was a friendly place, and I could not help but contrast the campus and comfortable old buildings of Johns Hopkins with the National Cancer Institute, full of busy scientists, housed in tall and sterile white government "modules."

Pat Walsh flashed a smile and greeted me warmly. He worked quickly, his words and movements crisp and efficient as he checked my prostate, stepped into the lab for a quick look at my pathology slides, and returned with the verdict.

"Dr. Hatcher did a nice work-up, Mr. Jordan. You

have a significant amount of cancer in your prostate. In my opinion, you should have it removed. If you like, I'll be glad to take it out."

If you like . . . I wanted to hug him. I had expected to be handed off to one of his bright young associates. My goal had been merely to get into "his" program. It was a wonderful bonus to know that he would perform "his" surgery on me.

He talked for a couple of minutes about the operation, the likely outcome and the risks. Patrick Walsh oozed confidence. Here was a man at the top of his game. "You've got a problem . . . I'm going to fix it," was his attitude.

At one level, he was totally professional, cool, and a bit detached. Yet he was capable of shifting gears and talked with feeling about "my patients," and at one point held up his somewhat delicate hands, which he described as "the gift God has given me" to perform surgery.

When Dr. Walsh told me that I would have to wait five weeks to have my surgery, my heart sank. With my first cancer, I had received my diagnosis late one Friday afternoon and convinced my doctors at NCI to allow me to start my chemotherapy the next day, which happened to be my forty-first birthday. I had no intention of giving my body the weekend off so the cancer cells could multiply while I was eating birthday cake.

But this was different. Dr. Walsh explained that the needle biopsy irritates the prostate and that it was important for the prostate gland to return to a "normal condition" before he performed the delicate surgery.

He reassured me that waiting a few weeks with my medium-grade cancer was not of great concern. Easy for him to say.

When I started to push for an earlier date, Dr. Walsh cut me off, saying quietly, "After doing many, many of these procedures, I believe it's best to wait."

I dropped it. "We" had decided to wait.

It was not easy to tell Dr. Hatcher — himself a great surgeon and researcher — that I was going to Johns Hopkins. Dr. Hatcher had encouraged my aggressive attitude, performed a random biopsy when my ultrasound was normal, and actively supported my efforts to consider all my options. His reaction was gracious and generous. He described Dr. Walsh as a "great surgeon" and said I had made an excellent decision. The important lesson I learned from Paul Hatcher is that great doctors are not threatened by patients seeking second opinions or going other places for their surgery . . . they are too busy taking care of their own patients and making their own miracles.

The surgery would take Dorothy and me away from our family for at least a week. We could get away with telling little Kathleen and Alex that "Daddy has to go get his prostate fixed," but that would not satisfy Hamilton Jr., who had sensed something was wrong and was already asking questions. Should we tell him everything . . . or the bare minimum to protect him from unnecessary worry? Dorothy wanted to tell him everything. I was not sure.

When the moment of truth came, I chickened out,

describing my surgery as a mechanical problem that many men face as they get older. He asked a couple of questions, ending with, "But you're going to be okay, for sure?"

"Yes, son, I'm going to be okay."

But, as usual, Dorothy was right, and within a few days, Hamilton had picked up on our anxieties and started asking questions again. I could not afford to lose his trust.

One night he drifted into my little office at home where I was on my computer. "Come on, son," I said, "let's take a walk."

It was a clear summer night, and we took turns pointing out the different constellations and stars. I put my hand on his shoulder, pulled him toward me, and looked him right in the eye. "Son, you are old enough to understand more about my prostate surgery." I paused, then plunged ahead: "The reason that I am having it removed is that they found some cancer in it."

His face dropped.

"But I have the best surgeon in the world who is going to take it out, and then it'll be done with."

Tears welled up in his eyes as he threw his arms around me and buried his head in my shoulder. "But will you be okay? Is there any chance that you will die in surgery?"

"No!" I stated emphatically and painted an optimistic picture, rattling off favorable statistics and stating that no person had ever died of prostate cancer surgery at

Johns Hopkins. (This was my guess, not a fact, and I remembered my mother's saying that "White lies, told to avoid hurting another person, are recorded by God in invisible ink.")

For the remainder of the summer, we tried to live a normal life while waiting for my surgery. We didn't keep my cancer a secret but neither did we broadcast it or let it dominate our lives. I didn't want to tell my friends until we had a more definitive, and we hoped, a more optimistic prognosis.

There was plenty to do to get ready. I had to donate several pints of blood to be used in my surgery, update my will, check on a couple of insurance issues, and organize my work since I would be out of commission for a while.

I also had to drink a lot of green tea. Sitting around for five weeks thinking about a single cancer cell escaping my prostate and traveling to some other part of my body was driving me crazy. So I had called a friend who is a distinguished molecular biologist and asked him if there were any known treatments or herbs that might help suppress prostate cancer while I waited for my surgery. He faxed me an interesting abstract about a study on "green tea" that was being conducted by scientists at the University of Chicago.

I called and talked with the principal researcher and got the basic pitch: Prostate cancer — the leading cause of cancer among American men — is almost nonexistent in many parts of Southern Asia. Some scientists have come to believe that the reason for this is the presence and frequent intake of "green tea," which contains naturally occurring catechins, believed to have anticancer properties which are active against prostate cancer.

I happened to mention this in a phone call to Tom Beard, an old and loyal college friend who had gone to Washington with the Carter administration and was and is widely known for his generosity. Several days later, a truck pulled into our driveway and a man came to our door with a "delivery."

"What is it?" I asked.

"Tea," the man replied.

"Where is it?" I asked, expecting to be handed a tin or small box of tea.

"Sir, it was too much for me to hand carry . . . it's in the truck. But I'll get it."

Pretty soon he had loaded up his trolley and had dumped it on our kitchen floor — sixty pounds of green tea!

I looked again at the scientific abstract from the University of Chicago. The study had implanted human prostate cancer in "nude mice" (mice without active immune systems) so that the cancer would be able to reproduce and grow rapidly without any immune-system resistance.

In the mice that had been given regular injections of these catechins derived from green tea, the prostate cancer had been stymied in its growth and in some cases the tumors had been melted away. There was no question that in mice implanted with human prostate cancer, the green tea had active anticancer properties.

I was disappointed, however, when I tried to duplicate the experiment and calculated that to drink as much as the mice in the study, I would have to imbibe about six gallons of the bitter green tea a day! Nevertheless, I still managed to put away six or seven cups of the awful-tasting stuff every day from the time it arrived to the morning we left for Johns Hopkins. At least it made me feel like I was doing something to fight my cancer while waiting for my surgery.

FINALLY, THE SURGERY

Our dear friend Sally Hale — who is executive director of Camp Sunshine — served as surrogate mom while we were away, much to delight of our children who adored their "Aunt Sally." But I read the concern on Hamilton Jr.'s face as we pulled out of the driveway and headed for the airport. "Something would be wrong with him if he wasn't worried," Dorothy said. She was probably right, but that did not make it any easier for me.

Dr. Walsh was especially attentive to Dorothy's concerns at our pre-surgical exam, talking about "your surgery" as if she were going under the knife with me. He explained his "system," the surgery, my hospital stay, and warned against being macho by trying to leave the hospital prematurely. "Finally, I am obligated to state the risks. You may have some short-term incontinence, which will resolve in time, so don't be discouraged. There is some risk of impotence, but most men in their early fifties usually do very well."

"That's no problem, Dr. Walsh. Dorothy already thinks that I'm impotent."

Dr. Walsh smiled. Dorothy blushed slightly and feigned a slap.

"One more thing, Dr. Walsh, would you be sure to note the exact color of my prostate when you remove it?"

"The color?" he asked with a quizzical look on his face. "What in the world are you talking about?"

As I told Dr. Walsh the story of the green tea, I could tell that he was struggling to keep a serious look on his face.

"How interesting!" he mumbled, as I saw him shoot a glance and raise an eyebrow to one of his young residents.

"Hamilton, I will certainly look to see if you have an Irish prostate because I have never seen one in the thousands that I have removed over the years."

I was not going to let him off that easily. I cited the serious research and said, "But Dr. Walsh, it stands to reason that the men who drink green tea would not have developed prostate cancer in the first place."

"You're right, " he said, failing to hide a bit of sarcasm in his voice and the twinkle in his eye. "I will be looking tomorrow for my first green prostate."

The night before my surgery, Dorothy and I tried hard to have a "romantic" evening with a seafood dinner at a cozy restaurant on the Baltimore Inner Harbor and a boat ride back to our hotel. While unspoken, the next day's event weighed heavily over us both.

I got up around 4:00 A.M., gave myself the required enema, and checked into the surgery waiting room at 6:30 A.M., already filled with patients and their families. The atmosphere in the small room was strained . . . some struggled to make small talk to pass the time while others just sat there alone with their thoughts. It was the longest two hours of my life, and I was relieved when a nurse finally called my name, led me into the "prep" room, and handed me the green hospital gown.

The only thing of mine left on was a Camp Sunshine "friendship bracelet" of fishhooks and beads made by a beautiful young camper named Tess Strickland, who had died in 1991. The last time I saw Tess, I told her that I would never take it off to guarantee that my wonderful memories of her would be with me forever. I started to explain, but a stout nurse (who reminded me of Nurse Ratched from *One Flew over the Cuckoo's Nest*) didn't want to hear about it. "Hospital rules," she barked, as she snapped it off. I had broken my promise to Tess, but I was sure she would understand.

Dorothy, a former nurse herself, tried to be helpful as they took my blood pressure, started my IV, and strapped me onto the surgical bed. "You don't know what you are doing," I complained jokingly and gave her a quick hug.

The nurse agreed. "It's time to go, Mr. Jordan . . . you don't keep Dr. Walsh waiting!"

"Get out of here, Doffy. I love you . . . see you in a few hours."

Dorothy turned at the door, and in a weak attempt to hide a tear, forced a smile, then disappeared.

I was ready to go. I was wheeled through the swinging doors of the operating room and immediately felt like I was in the middle of a football huddle, surrounded by men and women in masks and surgical garb leaning over me, talking in hospital jargon while connecting tubes and lines, and preparing me for my spinal block.

While the casual talk continued, the atmosphere changed the instant that Dr. Walsh appeared: "Good morning, ladies and gentlemen." He leaned over me and said, "Are you doing okay? We are going to take good care of you."

His few words made me feel like someone had poured an enormous bucket of confidence all over me.

He started giving directions in staccato fashion while I strained to listen and understand. It was quickly apparent that Dr. Walsh was not here just to supervise a young associate doing my surgery. He was "hands on," just like he was in the video tape. I was pleased but not surprised.

The lower part of my body was growing numb from the spinal block, and the sedative that was supposed to relax me was taking effect. I began to feel groggy and slip away, but struggled to keep my eyes open.

While I have the distinct memory of being awake for

major parts of the surgery, I remember almost nothing about it. Later, one of the young doctors enjoyed telling me that throughout the surgery I had mumbled statistics on prostate cancer. "About half of them were accurate," he kidded.

They wheeled me into the recovery room, where I dozed off and on. I was aware for the first time of all the tubes running in and out of my belly. I felt my hand being squeezed and knew instantly that Dorothy was there. I opened my eyes to her smiling face and started firing questions: Had she seen Walsh? Was the cancer confined to my prostate? Were my lymph nodes negative? She told me that everything was "great" and was still trying to calm me down when Dr. Walsh appeared in his surgical garb with his mask pulled down, smiling.

"Dr. Walsh," I almost yelled, "You did such a great job that Dorothy and I are going to have sex tonight!"

He laughed, grabbed my hand, and told us that my surgery had gone "extremely well" — the lymph nodes were normal and the cancer appeared to be confined to the prostate. I also learned that I had bled a lot, which Walsh dismissed as a minor bump in the road. "That's why it's good to have this surgery done by a team who has done hundreds of these operations . . . a little extra bleeding is no big deal."

Dr. Walsh said it would be several days before the final pathology reports were back. "I'll drop by and see you tomorrow in your hospital room because you will probably not remember what I just told you," he added.

But I remembered vividly every single word he had said. I dozed off and on in my hospital room for the rest of the day. Dorothy said I slept with a smile on my face. I was glad to have it over.

Once my head cleared, I wanted a good look at my incision, so I pulled up my gown and was shocked to find giant staples running the vertical length of my lower abdomen, over twelve inches.

"How in the world do you get those staples out?" I asked my nurse.

"What would you think?" she said.

"Not a staple remover?"

"Exactly!" she chuckled as she pretended to hold a giant pair of pliers over my belly.

I winced at the thought.

My hospital stay was "textbook" with no setbacks or complications. I got up and walked the morning after my surgery. Though I was slightly dizzy at first and a bit wobbly, it was a victory for me just to shuffle down the hall.

Dr. Walsh walked into my room beaming on my third day after surgery. "Clean margins, no lymph node involvement, I was able to save both nerves and no sign in the pathology of any presence of cancer cells outside of the prostate."

Dorothy squeezed my hand, carefully leaned over my chest to give me a quick kiss, and stood up and hugged Dr. Walsh, who was surprised and a bit embarrassed.

He gave me careful instructions on how to pace myself during recovery, to which we listened attentively. I told him how fortunate we were to have had him as our surgeon.

Just as he prepared to move on to see his next patient, I said, "Dr. Walsh, you forgot about the most important thing. . . . What about the color, Dr. Walsh?"

"The what?" he replied.

"What about my Irish prostate? Was it green?"

He laughed out loud. "Hamilton, you had the most normal-looking, normal-colored prostate that I have ever seen . . . not even a hint of green!"

I let him enjoy his laugh and will never know whether or not the green tea had helped, but it had been an important emotional crutch for me as I waited for my surgery and fretted about the chance of a stray cell wandering outside my prostate.

Waiting for me when I returned home was another article about the efficacy of green tea, sent to me by the researcher from the University of Chicago. When I read it, I realized for the first time that I had been drinking the wrong kind of green tea! The tea that I had been forcing myself to swallow had actually been processed in a way that removed most of the anticancer catechins.

I laughed at myself, but I never regretted that for five weeks, I at least had the powerful feeling that I was doing something personally to kill those prostate cancer cells.

We checked out of the hospital five days after the surgery. I was anxious to get home, but sensitive about how I would appear to my children, hobbling around with the Foley catheter (my constant companion for several weeks), which allowed the urine to flow from my bladder into a plastic bag while my urethra was on the mend. I didn't quite know how to explain this to my children, but three-year-old Alexander obviously got it because he told his classmates that "Daddy went on a trip and bought a tee-tee bag."

It was good to sit in my favorite chair, sleep in my own bed, and listen to the happy sounds of my children romping in and out of the house. Each day was a little bit better. Carrying my "tee-tee bag," I walked laps around the pool, adding a few each day until I was soon walking three miles. Four weeks after surgery, my catheter was removed. Although we had bought a good supply of Depends, I only needed them for a few days before regaining nearly total control of my bladder.

Once the prostate gland is removed, the only way to track the possible spread of prostate cancer cells is through the PSA test. Without a prostate, a man should have a PSA level of zero. If the PSA is above zero and/or begins to rise over time, it is a strong indication that somewhere in the body prostate cancer cells are loose, multiplying, and will eventually reappear.

Dr. Walsh highly recommended that an Atlanta urologist, Dr. Tony Malizia, follow my case. Tony —

like Dr. Walsh — is a great surgeon and doctor who truly cares for his patients.

Ten weeks after my surgery, I had a PSA test. When I got a message that the nurse from Dr. Malizia's office had called, I was all smiles.

"Mr. Jordan, this is Peggy. Your PSA is 0.00 . . . perfect. You'll need another one in three months."

I hugged Dorothy, who started jumping up and down and dancing around the house. We had expected good news, but it was great to know for sure.

I am no hero and suspect that my tolerance for pain is normal. While it was no cakewalk, the "radical retropubic prostatectomy" as performed by Dr. Walsh and his team at Hopkins is not difficult. On a scale of 1 to 10 (10 representing intolerable pain), I had expected the surgery to be a 7 or 8 after a doctor friend warned me that removing the prostate is more difficult than heart bypass surgery. But my surgery was a 2 or 3. The only time I really "hurt" was the first couple of times I stood and walked, but that passed quickly. I would rather have five prostate surgeries than undergo another round of chemotherapy.

I was ready to get off the Prostate Cancer Roller

Coaster. It was time to relax, think about something else for a change, and start living our lives all over again.

I slept like a baby that night.

CLINTON, CANCER, & ME

"May I speak to Mr. Jordan?"

"This is he."

"The White House is calling."

My first reaction was to wonder why in the world the White House would be calling me . . . followed by a rush of excitement . . . tempered ultimately by reality setting in and my chuckling quietly at myself.

I had been on the other end of this little game so many, many times so many years ago, and, yet, it had still worked on me.

While waiting for the call, I remembered something that our plain-spoken attorney general, Judge Griffin Bell, used to tell his staff at the Justice Department. "Don't ever, ever tell me, 'The White House' called, or 'the White House wants this,' or 'the White House insists on that.' The White House is a damned building . . . I work for the president of the United States. I didn't leave the U.S. Court of Appeals to answer to some nameless, low-level White House staff person and certainly not to take orders from a damned building!"

But, despite my experience, I was as vulnerable as anyone else to the mystery and wonder of the magic phrase, "The White House is calling."

A nice young man came on the phone, told me his name (I had never heard of him), and said he was calling from the White House Personnel Office. Then — with a not-too-subtle change in his voice — he turned real serious on me and said that he was "calling on behalf of President Clinton and Vice President Gore."

"The president and vice president," he intoned, "have discussed this matter and would consider it a great service to the country if you would accept appointment to the Board of the National Cancer Institute. This is a very important board that advises the president and the director of the National Cancer Institute on national policy."

I played along, thanked the earnest young man, said that I was "flattered" to be considered, and asked him to send me some information on this board.

I could, of course, just imagine the president and vice president huddled in the Oval Office, spending hours as they struggled to decide whom to appoint to the National Cancer Board, and then deciding on me as the best possible person in the country! Then, after serving on the board, I could imagine myself sitting in the Oval Office next to the large Kennedy Desk as I advised the president on cancer policy as he developed the federal budget.

As Garth in *Wayne's World* would say: "Not!"

I remember when the White House Personnel Office reported to me . . . with hundreds of important presidential appointments to make, including ambassadors to foreign countries and key positions in major departments and regulatory boards, all of which required Senate confirmation. But we also had literally thousands of appointments to positions on advisory boards like the National Cancer Board. Most of the decisions on these lower-level appointments were not even submitted to the president, other than in the form of a long list of names simply for his own information.

While there was some politics involved, these advisory boards were basically a sop to your supporters, who typically enjoy the honor of a local press release ("The White House announced today that Peoria resident Philip Joiner has been appointed to the Advisory Committee on National Monuments"), as well as a beautiful document, suitable for framing. The appointment might also involve a meeting once a year.

In the Clinton White House, I knew that political considerations were always paramount. Someone obviously had connected my interest and work in cancer to this appointment, and the likely suspects were Vice

President Gore's staff, who were obviously hard at work using the powers and perks of the vice presidency to solidify political support.

I had been working for more than ten years on various efforts to increase cancer research funding, speaking around the country and writing op-ed pieces. I had thought that the Clinton-Gore Administration might be particularly receptive to an increase in federal funding of cancer research. Clinton's mother had died of breast cancer and Gore's sister — at a young age — had died of lung cancer. It seemed to me that the Clinton-Gore Administration could and might do much more . . . if they only knew the facts.

A few months earlier, I had requested fifteen minutes on Vice President Gore's crowded schedule during a visit he made to Atlanta for some political event. I ended up with him in his hotel room at the end of a long day. It was almost 10:00 P.M., and I appreciated more than most how exhausted he must be. I quickly made my pitch, using large, emphatic charts.

I did not know Gore well. He was a young member of Congress when we arrived in Washington. The vice president wore the dark blue suit and white shirt like a uniform. He was obviously smart, took his position and himself very seriously, and sadly seemed to be trapped in this persona. Mutual friends had told me that Al Gore is very different from his public image and can be loose and charming in a private setting. But on this occasion, Gore was exhausted from a long day and anxious to conclude our meeting. Nevertheless, he was cordial and gave me his undivided attention for a few minutes as he sat erect in a folding chair for my presentation.

I told the vice president that one out of every two men and one out of every three women would have cancer in their lifetime, due to our aging population and the decrease in mortality from other diseases. (Mortality from heart disease and stroke was down 25 percent in just the past decade.)

"Consequently, Mr. Vice President, more and more folks will have cancer in their lifetimes. In fact, it is not wrong to say that we are facing an epidemic of cancer in our country, and we are not doing enough about it."

I went on to tell him that federal funding for cancer research — which for the past twenty-five years had been the mainstay of basic research — was at best flat and had actually declined slightly in real terms during the Clinton-Gore years.

"As a nation, we spend $14 billion a year for the space program, $9 billion on the FAA to have safe air travel (only one out of every fifteen million people will die from an air accident), $2 billion a year for a B-1 bomber, and only $2 billion to understand this disease, cancer, which will strike 40 percent of the people alive in our country today. Is two-tenths of a penny out of every tax dollar enough for cancer research? People will not think so when cancer strikes them or a loved one."

Gore was now taking notes. I stopped . . . there was no need for me to beat the vice president on the head with any more facts. The Clinton-Gore administration had not given cancer research a very high priority . . . and the vice president knew it.

Gore was a bit defensive but well informed on the budget implications, and he challenged me on a couple of the statements and statistics . . . which I answered to his apparent satisfaction. When I got through, he was silent for a moment as if waiting for me to ask him for something.

"And so what are you recommending, Hamilton?"

"Mr. Vice President, I am recommending that we do more than spend two-tenths of a penny out of every tax dollar to find a cure for a disease that will strike almost half of all living Americans. It's as simple as that, and any economic model that you can construct will demonstrate that it is cheaper to prevent cancer than to cure it and cheaper to cure it than not to cure it."

"Fair enough," he said. He thanked me for my time and asked for a copy of my presentation.

I heard nothing else from Gore about this and — of course — closely watched for news reports on cancer research funding. When the next federal budget was announced, there was indeed an increase in cancer research funding, which friends at NCI told me Gore had sponsored. But the next year brought a drop in funding that almost offset the increase and left those new programs funded in the past year in a difficult position.

My hopes for cancer funding — just like Clinton's presidency — were fading.

And now this call to be on some board . . . a fairly obvious attempt by some political operative to "make peace" with at least one of the Carter folks. I chuckled as I thought about the strange twist of events and how my casual relationship with Clinton had come full circle from his chasing me twenty-five years ago to my lobbying him on cancer funding.

PRESIDENTIAL WANNABE, 1975

I do not know Bill Clinton well, but it is not surprising that, as two young people about the same age from the deep South involved in national Democratic politics, we had crossed paths a long time ago.

I had first heard about this young "hotshot" from Jody Powell in 1974. Then-Governor Carter had landed a spot as chairman of the 1974 Democratic Campaign Committee, a gift from Democratic guru and party chairman Bob Strauss, who created the Campaign Committee to help Democratic candidates around the country and also to utilize the efforts of the new Democratic governors who had supported Strauss's mandate to rebuild the party after the McGovern debacle.

I had written Carter a detailed strategic memo mapping a road to the White House, and this role with the national party helped us to meet politically active people around the country and build a network of friends who would know who Jimmy Carter was.

So I was not surprised in the late fall of 1975 — as it became increasingly apparent that Jimmy Carter was emerging as one of two or three leading Democratic presidential candidates — that we would attract to our campaign politically active young people.

"You simply have to meet him, Hamilton," pressed Anne Wexler, a leading Democratic activist who had made an early commitment to the Carter campaign. "You will really like him. Besides, you ought to know him . . . he is going to be president someday!"

I winced when she said that. I wasn't worried about someday . . . I was worried about the Democratic primaries only a few months away. While I didn't know this up-and-coming young pol, I knew the type. They were everywhere: young people — always men or boys at that time in the political life of our country — who had a bad case of what I called "Student Council syndrome." They had spent all of their young lives running for some office or other and getting their pictures in the paper.

Once they got out of college, their next stage of self-gratification was real politics. They began to attach themselves to successful campaigns and ingratiate themselves with successful candidates. But it was always transparent that they wanted to be the candidate themselves. They didn't want to stuff envelopes or organize precincts; they were mostly interested in personal exposure, and they wanted to travel with the candidate or deal with the press. My experience was that most of these guys didn't ever make it to the big time.

Maybe this guy was an exception, but it was a little too much for me that one of these nerds was already telling people he was going to be president of the United States.

On the plus side, the fact that we were beginning to attract these young pols was an indication that Democratic "insiders" had begun to take Carter's candidacy seriously. I was confident that we would win the Iowa caucuses and had a good shot at winning New Hampshire. If we won in the Midwest and the Northeast and then beat George Wallace in Florida, it would be hard to deny us the party's nomination.

I put off meeting the self-proclaimed future president as long as possible, but Anne Wexler was an important person to us. I finally ended up at a burger joint in Georgetown, waiting close to an hour for him to arrive.

Finally I ordered and had started to eat when a tall, attractive young man with a boyish face appeared out of nowhere. He had perfectly coiffed hair and a full, pleasant smile, which he flashed as he looked me right in the eye.

"Hi, I'm Bill Clinton . . . it is a real pleasure to meet you. I am terribly sorry to be late, but I had a meeting with Senator Fulbright which ran over."

Name-dropper, I thought.

He sat down and focused his full attention on me. To his credit, he had done his homework on me and our campaign and made a couple of interesting comments on the presidential campaign. He had studied the entire field, knew the intricacies of the primary and caucus schedule, and the strengths and weaknesses of each candidate.

I began to talk about Jimmy Carter and his progressive record as governor of Georgia.

Clinton listened for a few minutes while munching on a heaping plate of French fries which he dipped in ketchup one at a time before lifting them up and lowering them into his mouth. He finally pushed the plate away, leaned forward, and started peppering me with questions. They were not frivolous questions, and he quickly guided the conversation from Carter personally to the central political issue of electability. With so many candidates and proportional representation, wasn't there a good chance for a "brokered convention" which would work against an "outsider" like Carter? What did the polls show in Iowa, New Hampshire, and Florida? Did we really have a chance to sell Carter to conservative white Southern Democrats over George Wallace? Who was helping us in Miami? And on and on.

He was well informed and obviously much more concerned with whether or not Carter could win than what he would do as president. Although I knew and resented the fact that he was charming my pants off, I found him very bright and interesting.

As we finished our meal, Clinton mentioned that he had to run to a meeting with George McGovern. I no longer thought that he was name-dropping. This young pol probably really did have an appointment to see McGovern.

Clinton went on to explain that he was considering a race for attorney general of Arkansas, that he thought he could win it and might even be unopposed in the general election. He then added, "I would like to spend some more time with Governor Carter personally before I endorse him."

I wanted to throw up when he said that, but simply nodded my head, realizing that he could be a real asset to us in his home state.

"Well, you could be tremendously importantly to us in Arkansas."

"Obviously I can help you most in my home state but I do have a network of friends all over the country," he said, quickly mentioning the names of leading young activists he had met at Georgetown University and Oxford. "So don't limit my help to just Arkansas. I have got to win this nomination for attorney general back home, but frankly, I believe that I can help you in a lotta places."

I was beginning to think that this young man was about as sharp a young pol as I had ever seen and didn't doubt for a moment that with his network he could help us tremendously.

"What I would like to do after meeting with Governor Carter is to publicly endorse him and send a letter to all my friends and contacts, explaining to them why I am supporting Carter and asking for their support." In a poor attempt at modesty, Clinton added, "I believe it might be a little help."

As I took a taxi back to the hotel, I could imagine the young politico returning to Arkansas, taking out his file box of contacts and putting down my name and address.

Clinton got his extended meeting with Carter, who was completely smitten. "He is one of the sharpest young persons I have ever met," Carter gushed. Carter urged me to get him involved in our campaign and to get his formal endorsement as soon as possible.

I called Clinton to follow up, and he indicated that he needed some time to "touch bases" with a few people but that he would get it done quickly.

As I continued to prod him over the next several months, Clinton was always "on the verge" of endorsing Jimmy Carter for president. When Carter asked what was going on, at first I covered for Clinton and told him it was "in the works," but was complicated by the fact that he was in the middle of a primary contest for attorney general. Finally, I told Carter the truth — that Clinton had simply not done what he had promised. Carter refused to believe that the impressive young man had let him down and blamed me for our "poor follow-up."

Clinton's long-awaited endorsement finally came through — after we were well on the way to winning the Democratic nomination. Still, it was a strong and effective endorsement. We all got a good chuckle over the fact that it grossly exaggerated Clinton's relationship with Carter, but that was just politics.

My voice dripping with sarcasm, I informed Carter that Bill Clinton had made a "courageous decision" to support him.

Carter playfully accused me of being "jealous."

By the summer of 1976, Bill Clinton had won the nomination for attorney general of Arkansas, was running unopposed in the general election, and was already being mentioned as a leading Democratic candidate for governor in the next election. He was clearly the best person to head up the Carter campaign in Arkansas, and the position was also highly compatible with his own ambitions, giving him an excuse through the fall of 1976 to do what he liked best . . . travel around the state, speak, and campaign. Clinton enthusiastically accepted the position and did a very good job.

As we organized that summer for the national campaign, an effort was mounted by some of the women in the campaign to install Clinton's new wife, Hillary, as campaign director for one of our key Midwest states.

Some found it strange that she would want to work outside of Arkansas — her political home and base — but it made sense to me. Clinton — as a 28-year-old Attorney General Democratic nominee without opposition — was already looking to make national contacts.

Our national field director interviewed her and reported that she was smart and savvy and had indicated an interest in running our state campaign in Illinois. It was hard to imagine Hillary Clinton, an avowed feminist with her own liberal agenda, working with Chicago's Mayor Daley, but she served as deputy director of our Indiana campaign and got high marks for her work.

When I met Hillary at a campaign training session, I was struck by her appearance. I had expected the handsome young politician to have an attractive, Junior League wife — kind of the Ken and Barbie of our political futures. Instead, a very serious woman who was strikingly plain shook my hand firmly while looking me in the eye and said, "I am Hillary Rodham."

I waited for "Clinton," but it never came.

She wore a sixties-style "granny gown" with her hair pulled back in a bun and dark, clunky glasses that were as thick as a Coke bottle. Her features were pleasant enough, but it was as if she wanted to create the impression that she did not give a damn how she looked. Hillary Rodham had been highly successful.

She used our brief encounter to mention that women throughout the country would be looking for signals as to whether Governor Carter was serious about equal opportunities for women. She pointed out that Carter's record in Georgia — while "respectable" — was not "outstanding." She told me — in a matter-of-fact way that was quite effective — that we did not have enough women in visible and important positions in the national campaign.

I was very impressed with Hillary Rodham, and thought about the powerful political duo she and her husband formed. I also thought that they should be living in California, New York, or Massachusetts. The combination of Bill Clinton's youth, her style, and their liberal views would not sit well in the conservative South.

In the years that followed, I realized that I had indeed earned a place in Bill Clinton's imagined "box." I got Christmas cards, invitations to his inauguration in Little Rock and — starting in the mid-1980s — invitations to "Renaissance Weekend," an annual gathering at Hilton Head Island over the Christmas holiday that was a thinly disguised platform for Clinton to meet and to show off for important people who might be useful in some future national effort.

By this point in his career, Clinton had already been handed his first statewide electoral defeat (for governor in 1980) and had gone into a personal funk. Arkansas acquaintances told me that he was having trouble absorbing his defeat, that he talked about it and relived it endlessly. Clinton found himself suddenly out of office with nothing to do and was recklessly chasing women. One Arkansas friend called it the "Animal House" period of Clinton's life.

But they also credited Hillary with "snapping him out of it" and getting him "back on track," which — to Bill Clinton — meant running for office again. He defeated the incumbent governor in 1982, and by 1986, Governor Bill Clinton was once again weighing a national race.

At the urging of South Carolina governor Dick Riley, Dorothy and I went to Renaissance Weekend over New Year's of 1986 — just when I was on the road to recovery from my lymphoma. It was the ultimate gathering of ambitious and politically active young professionals, jogging on the beach in the morning, reading the *New York*

Times while sipping their cappuccinos, debating the merits of various wines, and talking about trips to Sante Fe and Napa Valley. While speaking the language of populism, most exuded an air of elitism and self-importance.

Though the purpose of the weekend was transparent, it was well-organized and featured interesting topics and people. I was asked to participate in a panel with Admiral Elmo Zumwalt and a couple of other people. We were asked to share some "personal experience." The story the Admiral told was not new to me . . . but it touched me profoundly.

A hush came over the room as the silver-haired and fit old sailor, dressed in a dark gray suit and red tie, stood erect to address the group.

"Without knowing it," he began, "I was responsible for ordering the use of Agent Orange, a chemical that killed my son and many other peoples' sons. Now that I understand the impact of my decisions and the pain of so many other parents' loss, I have the responsibility to do something about it . . . nothing is more important to me."

Zumwalt went on to say that no one hates war more than the old commanders who are "sentenced" to spend the rest of their lives thinking of all the good young men in their command who were not able to live a full life. "It is the ultimate irony for me that my own son suffered because of a decision that I made on behalf of our country. I take small comfort in the fact that no one knew at that time the dangers associated with Agent Orange.

That sad fact does not bring back my boy to me nor anyone else's sons."

I then got up, talked about my illness and almost felt compelled to mention my own time in Vietnam and exposure to Agent Orange . . . as if to underline the importance of Admiral Zumwalt's message and efforts. I looked over to the side where the admiral was seated and saw him dabbing his eyes with a white handkerchief.

After hearing my story, the distinguished old seaman walked up, hugged me, and said, "I am very, very sorry that you have this terrible disease."

I was deeply touched by his words and physically comforted by the strong arms stiffly wrapped around my shoulders. I knew he was thinking about his son. . . . I almost felt guilty about my own good prognosis. Tears trickled down my face and I tried to speak, wanted to say something that might be comforting . . . but could not. Admiral Zumwalt seemed to understand.

"He'll never be president," I told my wife after we returned from Renaissance Weekend. "Clinton's ambitions ooze out of every pore. It is all so transparent. The only thing he really believes in is himself."

In 1988, Bill Clinton was chosen to be the "keynote speaker" at the Democratic National Convention. Historically, the "keynote address" is broadcast in prime time and sets the tone and theme for the convention. Surprisingly, Clinton misread his audience, thinking that they wanted to hear from him as much as he wanted to be heard. He talked on and on and on, the twenty-minute speech dragging on for over fifty minutes. The network anchors started to make snide comments and cut away for commercial breaks while Clinton was still speaking. Having totally lost the crowd, Clinton's biggest applause came when he said, "In closing," and the conventioneers spontaneously erupted.

I enjoyed watching the well-deserved humiliation of this overly ambitious young man. It was clear that whatever remote possibility he had of national office was dashed that night.

A couple of nights later, smarting from pundits' comments and jokes on late-night television, Bill Clinton was on the Johnny Carson show, playing the saxophone and poking fun at himself in a carefully calibrated mea culpa. It didn't matter . . . it was too late.

Bill Clinton would never be president.

PRESIDENT CLINTON

Once again, Clinton had done what I thought was impossible. Had I continually underestimated him and Hillary because my judgment was flawed? Or was I simply envious at some level — for myself or for Jimmy Carter — over Clinton's polished and practiced political skills?

While I didn't care for him, some Democratic friends started lobbying right after his election for me — as the only former chief-of-staff of a living ex-Democratic President — to meet with the leadership of the Clinton transition team. I was never sure if they were really trying to help or simply hoping to ingratiate themselves with the Clinton team by "brokering" the Carter political family through me.

I remembered warmly the many kindnesses shown us by Dick Cheney and the Ford Administration as we prepared to take office — even though we had just defeated President Ford in a very close, highly partisan election.

In that campaign, Jimmy Carter had pledged that there would be no powerful chief-of-staff in his White House — which was compatible with the way Carter had done business as governor of Georgia and compatible with the post-Watergate mood of the country. One of the sad legacies of the Nixon White House was that his top staff — and in particular H. R. "Bob" Haldeman — had helped to create an atmosphere that isolated Nixon and that allowed and even encouraged some of their reckless and illegal activities.

Upon replacing Nixon, President Ford had vowed to run the White House without a chief-of-staff, using a "spokes of the wheel" concept with a number of senior aides (the "spokes") all reporting to the president (the "hub") personally. But it did not take long for President Ford and his senior staff to understand that this would not work, and he remedied the problem by appointing the very popular and capable congressman Richard Cheney to be his chief-of-staff. When he accepted the appointment, the senior staff members of the White House gave Cheney a bicycle wheel, spokes all broken, to symbolize the end of the failed management scheme and the staff's support for a more centralized system for operating the White House.

The first time I met Cheney in the large corner office (which would soon be my office), he was warm and gracious with his advice and help. He finally told me that he realized that Carter had made a campaign promise not to have a chief-of-staff and it was probably impossible to change his mind, but that the modern presidency needed a chief-of-staff. I listened carefully, and then tried to explain Carter's thinking without sounding defensive. I told him that I would convey his feelings to the new president, which I did shortly thereafter in a memorandum that followed. I was not surprised when Carter put a large "C" in the corner of the cover page, which meant that he had read the memo, had no comment, and obviously had not changed his mind. There would be no "powerful chief-of-staff" in the Carter White House.

When the call came – twelve years later – to meet with President-elect Clinton's staff, I put aside my own personal feelings and tried to think how I could offer suggestions and advice that might help the new president and his team to be successful, hopefully in the same spirit and nonpartisan tradition that Dick Cheney had helped me.

However, I was quickly reminded that politics was still the determining factor when I was invited to come to Little Rock and meet with a "key person" (unnamed) of the Clinton transition team on a "very confidential basis" — meaning, "Please don't tell anybody because the last thing in the world we want is for the press to write we are taking advice from Jimmy Carter's people!"

After vowing to keep our meeting quiet, I flew into Little Rock on a brisk fall day, was met by a banker friend who set it up and taken to his offices downtown. Once again, I had my big charts prepared for the presentation.

In a few minutes, a slight young man, dressed casually in slacks and a sweater hurried in, stuck out his hand, and said, "Hello, I'm George Stephanopolous."

He was friendly, intelligent, and to the point. It didn't take me long to suspect that someone had made him come to meet me — probably against his will — and that he was only going through the motions, feigning interest but not very convincingly.

Later I would learn that he was a former congressional staffer who had played a key role in Clinton's campaign and would serve the president first as press secretary and eventually as a very key political adviser.

I realized that I was wasting my time and rushed through my presentation. He seemed to take a few notes (or maybe doodled), and asked a couple of perceptive questions. The meeting ended quickly.

While I was putting my presentation boards into the large black carrying case, I said, "George, you probably have gotten more free advice than you need or can use, but if you don't do anything else, get rid of the Independent Counsel law. It is a bad law!"

"Oh really?" Stephanopolous said. "Is that because of your personal experience?"

Touché, I thought.

"Yes, George, it is because of my personal experience, but also because it will bite your administration in the ass just like it did our administration and Reagan's and Bush's."

He assured me that they would have someone look into it, shook my hand, told me he appreciated my coming, and quickly departed.

On the way back to the airport, my banker friend who had arranged the meeting asked if the young Clinton aide had learned anything.

"About as much as I learned when I was briefed the first time by President Ford's chief-of-staff, Dick Cheney."

"Was that a lot?" he asked.

"There was a lot for us to learn from Dick Cheney and the Ford folks . . . we just didn't pay any attention to them. Every administration thinks the challenge of the presidency will be different for them, and that they are smarter than whomever they are succeeding."

BILL & JIMMY

Later on, pundits and commentators would come to describe the Clinton-Carter relationship as "rocky" and "complicated." While it was certainly "rocky," it was not that complicated to me.

Jimmy Carter had done what Clinton had always wanted to do . . . be the first president since the Civil War from the Deep South. Once Carter had been defeated and Washington insiders talked about our "failed presidency," Clinton and his people went to extremes to be "not Jimmy Carter."

While at a practical political level I understood what was going on, at a personal level I did not like it. When Clinton actually won the presidency, I and others close to the Carters deeply resented their treatment at the Clinton inauguration, where the new president and First Lady went so far as to celebrate the Reagans in public ceremonies while ignoring the Carters, who had enthusiastically supported Clinton in his campaign for president.

President Carter had learned early on in his presidency the value of keeping former presidents well-informed on political issues, particularly foreign policy. For example, by keeping former presidents Nixon and Ford informed about the negotiations on the Panama Canal Treaties, the Camp David Accords, and the SALT Treaty (Strategic Arms Limitations), President Carter had earned their public support for his policies. In turn, both Presidents Reagan and Bush had briefed Carter regularly and gotten — in return — Carter's support and help on a number of controversial issues.

But the Clinton administration did a poor job of keeping former president Carter informed.

At the same time, the non-profit Carter Center had established an international reputation around the world, focused on important works ranging from human rights and free elections to disease eradication. But the Carters were denied access to basic information that would enable them to pursue and support the objectives of the Clinton State Department and White House. Conversely, the Clinton administration failed to utilize the first-hand perspective the Carters had derived from their travels, their good works around the world, and their interactions with key leaders.

Over time, President and Mrs. Carter became more willing to take personal risks and exploited opportunities to become personally involved in mediating disputes in hot spots like North Korea, Panama, and Haiti without exposing the Clinton administration to the public perception of a setback or policy failure.

Clinton — having failed to keep Carter in the policy loop — paid the price by having a very respected, high-profile Jimmy Carter traveling around the world working on his own priorities. The Carters kept the White House and State Department informed of their activities, but it was a one-way street, the result being that President Carter felt less and less of an obligation to espouse the Clinton line on critical policy issues.

MISSING IN ACTION:
THE NATIONAL CANCER ADVISORY BOARD

I never accepted nor turned down the appointment that the Clinton-Gore administration offered me and still have the thick stack of disclosure forms to be filled out sitting on my desk.

I toyed with the idea of accepting the appointment merely because I thought it might give me some additional clout to advocate increases in medical research funding. However, I didn't like the idea of anyone thinking that they could buy my political support or silence me by an appointment to an advisory board, particularly when the Clinton-Gore administration — touched in such a powerful way by cancer in their immediate families — had done so little. (In his campaign for president in 2000, Gore has pledged to double the size of the budget for cancer research . . . good for him!)

"The White House" kept calling — asking me to complete the forms so that I could be "officially appointed" to serve on the National Cancer Advisory Board. I put them off, blaming the delay on the long and complicated disclosure forms that pry into every element of your personal and business life, the kinds of questions that many claim discourage good people from serving.

I decided that a better use of my time would be to continue to work directly with cancer patients and provide the kinds of specific advice that are included in the self-help section at the end of this book.

SWEET IRONY

The rich irony of life has made many of my experiences live on in powerful ways.

WALTER CRONKITE

Years later, my old colleague Jody Powell shared an elevator ride with Walter Cronkite after an event at the National Press Club.

Cronkite inquired about my health and volunteered that he thought the worst story that he had ever broadcast at CBS News was the story on my alleged use of cocaine. "Hamilton Jordan was treated very unfairly," Cronkite told Jody.

It was good to learn that this great and honorable newsman had acknowledged a mistake. Tens of millions of people had seen or heard the original story about me by Mike Wallace. Much later, only Jody and a few others in the elevator heard Walter Cronkite's expression of regret.

KATHERINE GRAHAM

A couple of years after leaving Washington, I served on a nonprofit board with Katherine Graham, owner of the *Washington Post*, and she became my friend.

When Dorothy and I were in Bethesda during my treatment for lymphoma, Kay hosted a dinner party for us at her Georgetown home. She invited everybody who was anybody in Washington and proposed a toast.

Kay got up and made some nice comments about me, saying pointedly that it had been fun getting to know me after I had left Washington. Raising her champagne glass, she said, "To Dorothy and Hamilton, welcome to the Establishment!"

I got up and responded by saying that if she had hosted this dinner for me in the late 1970s, maybe I would not have had to leave. My suggestion that I had erred by not embracing the Washington Establishment was well received.

KING, CLARENCE & CARTER

Martin Luther King Jr. is buried at the King Center, not far from the State Capitol in Atlanta.

Jimmy Carter, who only got a handful of black votes in his successful campaign for governor, made history in his inaugural address when he stated simply that "The time for racial discrimination is over." That straightforward declaration — never heard in the South and long overdue — was followed by immediate action in integrating state government, an action that catapulted Carter onto the cover of *Time* magazine. This important work alienated many of his white supporters in Georgia but was a significant first step in Carter's progress toward becoming a national political figure.

There are only two portraits hanging in the Georgia Senate Chamber. One is of Jimmy Carter, a member of that Senate from 1962 to 1966. The other is that of my grandfather, Hamilton McWhorter, who — while progressive for his time — was an avowed segregationist. President of the Georgia Senate in the 1930s, he ended his political career — and sacrificed a chance of becoming governor of Georgia — when he married my grandmother, a pretty young Jewish girl.

One hundred miles south of Atlanta on the grassy slopes of Koinonia, Clarence Jordan is buried in an unmarked grave. It has been thirty years since Clarence's death, and a lot of people have come and gone in that time. A few oldtimers can walk you over to where they think Clarence is buried, but as the years pass and memories fade, opinions as to the exact location are beginning to differ.

I am sure that Clarence does not care.

A few miles down the road in Americus, Georgia — which for fifty years was a hotbed of racism and radical conservatism — Habitat for Humanity, which was Clarence's dream, has its international headquarters. Built upon the simple notion that a family needs a home to have pride, stability, and a chance in life, Habitat has become an important force for good throughout the world.

Millard Fuller, a wealthy young businessman who gave away all of his worldy goods and moved his family to Koinonia to follow Clarence, is now Habitat's Executive Director. Jimmy and Rosalynn Carter are two of its most visible volunteers.

I had often wondered if the Carters were trying to make up for the years they were not able to openly support Clarence. However, in a recent conversation, President Carter told me that the Carter warehouse was in fact boycotted for helping Koinonia. "But we never did anything heroic," added the former president.

ANDREW YOUNG

The light-skinned black man ("high yellow" in those days) whom I so clearly remember marching down

Pine Avenue arm-in-arm with Dr. King in Albany, Georgia, turned out to be Andrew Young, whom President Carter appointed to be our nation's first black United Nations ambassador.

Andy lost his first wife, Jean, prematurely to cancer. Having long been friends with him, I gave him one of my little cancer booklets, which prompted him to begin to have his prostate checked regularly with my local urologist. A recent checkup revealed a "rising PSA," and Andy was diagnosed with prostate cancer. But — like me — he caught it early, has had a successful surgery and has an excellent prognosis.

AGENT ORANGE & ADMIRAL ZUMWALT

President Clinton announced in 1998 — with Admiral Elmo Zumwalt at his side — that non-Hodgkins lymphoma and prostate cancer would be added to the list of diseases associated with exposure to Agent Orange in Vietnam for which veterans could now claim benefits. He gave Zumwalt credit for his efforts to bring this problem to the public's attention and for taking care of his soldiers.

I had thought that the risk of my being killed ended when I was evacuated from Vietnam following the 1968 Tet offensive. It obviously did not. I recently found an old photograph I had taken at a heliport in Vietnam that included in the background some of those 55-gallon drums with their characteristic orange markings. As I

AGENT ORANGE BARRELS IN TAN AN;
PHOTO TAKEN BY ME IN 1967, RECENTLY DISCOVERED

strained to read the writing on the drums, I could not help but wonder if those big cannisters of herbicide were the very drums of Agent Orange — containing dioxin — that started me along my long journey with cancer.

Admiral Zumwalt died of cancer himself in January 2000.

IRAN & THE HOSTAGE CRISIS

Almost every person who touched or was touched by the Iranian hostage crisis suffered some misfortune or tragedy:

• Omar Torrijos, who allowed the Shah to enter Panama from the United States, where he was hospitalized as a personal favor to me and President Carter and as a way to alleviate the hostage crisis, was killed in a suspicious plane crash. Many suspect that his plane was sabotaged by his ambitious security chief, Manuel Noriega, who seized power after Torrijos's death and ruled until the United States invaded Panama in December 1989. He was removed from power and put in jail for massive drug trafficking;

• Anwar Sadat, who was the only head of state in the world who would allow the Shah to come to his country when he left Panama, was killed by an assassin;

• Iranian Foreign Minister Sadegh Ghotzbadeh, who had been with Khomeini from the earliest days of his exile from Iran, risked his life twice by meeting secretly

IN THE OVAL OFFICE, TOASTING THE RELEASE OF THE AMERICAN HOSTAGES

with me in Paris to negotiate an end to the hostage crisis. Out of step with some of the radical elements of the movement, he was tried and executed by the very revolution that he had helped to start. The Ayatollah Khomeini did nothing to stop his execution.

• The Shah died in Egypt of complications from surgery to remove his spleen, grossly enlarged from his cancer;

• Jimmy Carter was defeated for re-election, the hostage crisis a major factor in his defeat;

• The two great historical figures in this struggle for the future of Iran — the Shah and Khomeini — died of non-Hodgkins lymphoma and prostate cancer, respectively, the exact cancers that I have had and — I hope — survived.

ANOTHER CAMP SUNSHINE?

Once again, Dorothy and I are involved in starting a special camp for children . . . this time for youngsters with juvenile diabetes. Our daughter, Kathleen, who was diagnosed with juvenile diabetes two years ago at the age of nine, will be able to attend. Juvenile diabetes lasts for a lifetime and gives you not a single day, or even afternoon, off. It is a tremendous management challenge: two or three shots every day; pricking your finger at least five times a day to check glucose levels; and carefully calculating the carbohydrates in every snack and meal. But it has turned into a character builder for our brave and spirited daughter.

ROSALYNN & JIMMY CARTER

President and Mrs. Carter have continued to be very active in the life of our country and our world.

While supporting them enthusiastically and taking a special pride in their good works, I do not agree with every single thing that President Carter does or says. But I do know that he and Rosalynn wake up every morning with the single thought: What can we do to make life a little bit better for some individual or group of disadvantaged or needy people?

Their most obvious and highly publicized work has been bringing democracies to other countries and President Carter's high-level interventions in "hot spots" like North Korea, Haiti, and Panama. Unknown to most people is the work of the Carter Center in health issues, particularly in Africa where — with the Carter's personal intervention — terrible diseases like Guinea worm and river blindness have been reduced from 3.5 million cases to less than 70,000, almost to the point of extinction.

Through word, deed, and example, the Carters have made an enormous difference in the world. Not enough, however, for me to ever get used to or to accept the bittersweet compliment, "Jimmy Carter is our greatest ex-president."

OUR LIVES

Except for my public work on cancer, Dorothy and I live a very quiet life in Atlanta. Every once in a while at an airport or restaurant, someone will come over and ask, "Didn't you used to be Hamilton Jordan?" Sometimes they call me "Jody"; other times they think they recognize me but aren't sure why. Some guess that I am a weatherman . . . others a football coach.

Occasionally, some over-forty stranger will make a good-humored wisecrack about my using cocaine or say, "I really liked that comment you made about the pyramids." I used to try to convince these people that these stories which amused them were not true.

I don't even respond anymore. . . . I just smile and try to change the subject.

Life is too short!

On the health front, I have regular checkups for my various cancers and listen to my body more closely than most. Fear is not logical, and no phantom or unexplained pain is ignored by me.

When and if another cancer shows up, I will be ready mentally, emotionally, and physically to beat it.

POSTSCRIPT:

CANCER, A STRANGE BLESSING

Although I have had three different cancers by age fifty, I do not feel cursed or put upon. Instead, I believe that I am very blessed and just plain lucky to be alive. I told my doctor that I do not mind having a new cancer every five years as long as he could guarantee me four or five more!

Sooner or later in life, we will all get a "bad report," which forces us to come to grips, probably for the first time, with our own mortality. Happily, this does not happen to most people until they reach their sixties or seventies.

But for those of us who are younger and survive a "bad report," a life-threatening disease like cancer is a strange blessing that casts our life and purpose in sharp relief. Some cancer patients allow cancer to dominate and define their lives. They cut themselves off from their families and friends, throw in the towel emotionally, expect the worst, and fulfill that expectation.

But there are many, many more who use their illness to find new meaning in their lives. And these are the patients who beat cancer against all odds or greatly exceed their prognosis or medical expectation.

While the memories of my three cancers are still vivid today, sometimes unsettling, and occasionally even frightening, I never want to forget the raw fear of cancer and the prospect of death. Because, if I am ever able to simply block out those memories and set my emotions aside, I will lose the ironic blessing, the sense of purpose and the focus that cancer has given my own life.

After my first cancer, even the smallest joys in life took on a special meaning — a beautiful sunset, a hug from my child, a laugh with Dorothy. That feeling has not diminished with time. After my second and third cancers, the simple joys of life are everywhere and are boundless, as I cherish my family and friends and contemplate the rest of my life, a life that I certainly do not take for granted.

Or, as my friend who is bravely battling a recurrent brain tumor reminds me, "There is no such thing as a bad day!"

PART TWO

WHAT CAN YOU DO
TO BEAT CANCER?

The three most feared words in the English language are: "You have cancer."*

In the United States and most Western cultures, the word "cancer" is synonymous with death — sometimes harsh and swift, sometimes long and drawn out, but almost always fatal.

This fear, along with the perception that cancer means "certain death," is widespread — *in spite of the fact that 50 percent of all cancer patients in the United States are cured of their illness!* And the cure rate can be expected to rise

---

*In a number of open-ended national surveys, when asked, "What is your greatest personal fear?" people ranked "cancer" or "public speaking" as their first or second greatest fear. When offered specific fears as choices, "cancer" was clearly number-one.

steadily (and possibly dramatically) over the next twenty years as progress is made in early detection, prevention through genetic screening of those with risk factors, and exciting new therapies that can only be imagined today.

While the belief that "cancer is a certain death sentence" may be irrational, the fear of the disease itself is not, as a significant number of us alive today will have cancer: *One out of every two men and one out of every three women living in the United States today will have cancer in their lifetime.* This is a staggering figure and one that is not understood by most Americans.

These statistics are based largely on our aging population, dramatic decreases in mortality from other diseases (like heart attack and stroke), and possible environmental impacts that we do not yet fully understand and cannot accurately measure.

Consequently, there is hardly a family or school or workplace that has not been or will not be touched by this disease.

MY JOURNEY

My own long journey with this disease began in 1982 when my wife started Camp Sunshine, which was one of the first camps for children with cancer in the country. Ironically, several years after we started Camp Sunshine, I had the first of three different cancers I would experience by the age of fifty.

I tell people that I have had "one of each" — a lymphoma that led to my taking experimental, industrial-strength chemotherapy; a bout with prostate cancer which required major and delicate surgery; and an early skin cancer that was dealt with simply and swiftly with a flick of the surgeon's knife and a couple of stitches.

While most cancer patients have the choice to deal with their illness quietly or openly, I did not have that luxury. Having left national politics only a few years earlier (or, more accurately, having been asked to leave by the American people in significant numbers!), I was in the twilight of a career in the public eye when I was diagnosed with my first cancer in 1985 (non-Hodgkins lymphoma).

I can remember like it was yesterday sitting in my hospital room with my family awaiting my pathology report and diagnosis and being staggered by a television news report that said I had "inoperable lung cancer."

Despite the wild inaccuracy of the report, I quickly learned that having been "outed" as a cancer patient by the news media was truly a blessing, as family and friends and people I did not even know came out of the woodwork to express their feelings for me and to offer help, support, and prayers.

While undergoing my first cancer treatment, I began to write and speak to groups of patients and lay people and found great comfort in doing so. I may have been bald and bloated from my chemotherapy, but this interaction with others who might benefit from my experience made me feel useful, and their courage and example strengthened my spirit, my body, and my resolve to live. It also made me a better person. Instead of focusing totally and selfishly on myself, these interactions with cancer patients — many of whom did not survive — made me acutely aware that (in the words of a friend with a brain tumor) "There's no such thing as a bad day."

After my second cancer, I wrote a little booklet, *Cancer: The Second Time Around*, which I distributed with such evangelistic zeal that friends started calling me "Johnny Appleseed."

The purpose of my little booklet was and is to encourage people to listen to their bodies, to get their annual physicals, and to "take charge" of their situation when diagnosed with cancer — or any other serious, life-threatening disease. Each of my three cancers was diagnosed early as a result of regular screening and aggressive follow-up. At last count, I have distributed almost ten thousand copies of my booklet and have had the joy of seeing the hard lessons I learned help other cancer patients take charge of their medical care.

By the late 1990s, I was getting more than ten calls a week about cancer from a growing number of people who had heard me speak somewhere, or had read my booklet, or had learned about my experiences from other cancer patients. It can be time-consuming and inconvenient to interrupt a family dinner or business meeting to talk with a newly diagnosed patient, but I tell my wife and friends, "What better way to spend fifteen minutes than giving anxious cancer patients advice and hope that might help them to save their own life?"

MY BELIEF

It is the premise of these pages and my strong belief that how people react — emotionally, intellectually, and physically — to the simple words "You have cancer" has a lot to do with whether or not they will live or die.

I know many strong and intelligent people who are so devastated by their diagnosis of cancer that they are paralyzed with fear, fail to take charge of their lives and medical options, and do not take advantage of their greatest resources:

> • The ability to be an active partner in the medical decisions that will determine whether they will live or die, and

> • The will to live, which now has been demonstrated scientifically to have an impact on the course of disease generally and cancer specifically.

I have never presumed to tell cancer patients what to do about their illness and treatment and always remind them that — like them — I am only a lay person, not a trained medical professional. But I never hesitate to tell them what questions to ask and the process to follow that will give them the best chance of being cured and living a quality life.

The section that follows is a practical guide — in abbreviated form — to the information that I have gathered about cancer, information I think might be most helpful to other cancer patients. Over the past two decades, I have dealt with hundreds of cancer patients and hundreds of physicians and nurses. Out of this experience, I have developed some strong feelings, ideas, and specific advice that many cancer patients have told me are very valuable.

CLOSING

I have never been able to think of cancer in the abstract and am only able to think of cancer in terms of its specific challenge and threat to the life of a fellow human being. While Dorothy and I have never allowed cancer to either define or dominate our lives, it has — for better or worse — been an important part of our existence for the past two decades.

For reasons that I have never been able to understand, people who have cancer are a remarkable group of brave, unselfish, and caring people. Maybe these people are changed forever by coming in touch with their own mortality, because the cancer patients I have known and cared about over the years are a remarkable group of human beings with a great spirit and a zest for living.

This book has been written for them and the many good people — sadly all around us — who will someday hear these frightening words "You have cancer," in the hope that my own journey and story might help them to be one of the ever-increasing number of survivors.

TOP TEN TIPS
FOR CANCER PATIENTS

Imagine that you have had an annual checkup, a nurse has called you back for "additional tests," and several days later, you find yourself sitting on a cold-metal examination table watching your doctor line your X rays up on a viewer, then pointing to a cloudy gray area on the film, and finally turning to utter the dreaded words, "I am sorry to tell you this, but I believe that you have cancer."

In response to this dire news, many people go into free-fall, they lose their perspective and good judgment, and they stumble through the next several days or weeks — *when critical medical decisions must be made* — without any knowledge or context for understanding their situation. Not always, but sometimes — and too many times in my own experience — cancer patients do not receive the best treatment from the best clinicians simply because of a lack of information.

We live at a time in history when all the knowledge of humankind is arguably at our fingertips.

However, while most Americans know where the carburetor is in their cars and how much RAM they have on their computers, very few of us know where our liver or kidney is or what its function is in our bodies.

The following "Top Ten Tips" provide a practical tool for cancer patients and their loved ones that will help them to synthesize the implied and explicit "lessons" from my story into very specific steps aimed at giving them the information they need to get the finest medical care possible with the best possible chance for being cured.

TIP #1

BE AN ACTIVE PARTNER IN THE MEDICAL
DECISIONS THAT ARE MADE ABOUT YOUR LIFE!

You cannot be an active partner in your medical care unless you understand your cancer. Everybody with normal intelligence can understand their illness, their choices and can make good decisions that enhance their chances for being cured and/or living a longer quality life.

If I had simply accepted the first advice given me by doctors, I would not have lived long enough to have a second or third cancer.

With my first cancer, my doctors were going to treat me for "local disease" with radiation. I later discovered from a more sophisticated, albeit old-fashioned test that my cancer had already spread throughout my body and that I needed to be treated systemically with experimental chemotherapy.

With my prostate cancer, the nurse in charge of giving me my annual test results understandably dismissed the higher reading on my PSA test because it was still within the "normal" range. However, because of the prostate cancer in my family (my father, my mother's father, three of my four uncles), I was not about to dismiss the results. I went to a urologist and insisted on a biopsy of my prostate, which revealed an early but aggressive prostate cancer. I quickly arranged for surgery to have my prostate removed, and the operation was a success. But if I had waited a year for another PSA test, the prostate cancer would likely have spread outside my prostate, making it "incurable."

TIP #2
SEEK AND KNOW THE TRUTH ABOUT YOUR ILLNESS AND YOUR PROGNOSIS.

Doctors told our grandparents the absolute minimum about their illnesses, being deliberately vague about their true condition and avoiding the use of the word "cancer" whenever possible.

Doctors today tell patients some version of "the truth." You must determine how much of that truth you want and can tolerate. My attitude was that crucial decisions were being made about *my life*. . . . I wanted all the facts and all the information available — even when that "truth" was unsettling.

This means asking questions, talking to other cancer patients who have had your disease, getting on the Internet or going to the library, and developing an understanding of your particular cancer.

However, do not ask questions if you are not prepared for the answers. I have seen "the truth" paralyze otherwise smart and sophisticated people because they could not handle being told that they had a 20 percent or even 50 percent chance of being alive in five years.

Some people are comfortable with their doctors making treatment decisions and choices for them. If that works for those people, we should respect and accept those choices. However, my experience is that decisions will be better decisions if the patient is well informed and actively involved.

TIP #3
GET A SECOND OPINION. IF THAT SECOND
OPINION IS DIFFERENT FROM YOUR FIRST OPINION,
GET A THIRD AND POSSIBLY EVEN A FOURTH.

We demand choices and options in every area of our lives: young people apply to numerous colleges; people get competitive bids for house plans, construction loans, and mortgages; and job seekers interview for several jobs. Most of us have several relationships before deciding whom to marry.

But when it comes to making literal life-and-death decisions about cancer treatments, patients far too often are willing to accept the first option offered.

By seeking second and even third opinions, you will either develop a consensus among your doctors as to what you should do (and have the comfort of having uniform advice); *or* you will have options and decisions to make. If your doctor actively discourages or opposes your getting a "second opinion," get another doctor. His or her attitude suggests either that he or she suffers from professional insecurity or that he or she is trying too hard to hang onto you as a patient.

It is a physician's professional obligation to furnish your records, X rays, and pathology reports to other doctors and institutions for a "second opinion." Sometimes these opinions are simply a matter of reading existing X rays or pathology reports and do not require an office visit or trip to another city. I always chose to get my "second opinion" *in person* so I could look the doctor in the eye, evaluate him or her in person, and have my questions answered.

TIP #4

DETERMINE UP-FRONT HOW BROAD OR HOW NARROW YOUR PHYSICIAN'S EXPERIENCE IS IN TREATING YOUR SPECIFIC TYPE OF CANCER, PARTICULARLY IF DIFFICULT PROCEDURES AND/OR NEW TREATMENTS ARE INVOLVED.

After my prostate cancer, I distributed my little booklet to friends on my Christmas card list. I got a call from a college friend, Paul, who lives in a small town in Georgia. He had discovered that he had early prostate cancer and was a prime candidate for a "radical prostatectomy," the same procedure I had, which promises a high cure rate and a greatly reduced incidence of incontinence and impotency.

But it is a very difficult and precise surgical procedure. The patient is opened from "the front," which allows the surgeon to operate in a "bloodless field," checking for the possible spread of cancer and separating intact the tiny nerves from the prostate that control the bladder and sexual function, and then carefully removing the diseased prostate. This procedure is only ten years old, and a relatively small number of surgeons have done more than fifty operations a year for more than five years — my definition of broad and long experience.

My friend called to thank me for the booklet, which had prompted his early diagnosis, and mentioned that the urologist at the local hospital was going to perform the new "radical prostatectomy" on him. "What do you think about that?" he asked.

I suggested that he determine how many of these difficult procedures his urologist had performed and how frequently he had done them.

Paul called back to say that his urologist had only done ten of these procedures in his career, the most recent six months earlier. With no prodding from me, Paul knew immediately that he needed someone more experienced, made arrangements to go to a highly experienced prostate surgeon, tolerated the surgery, and is free of disease today and doing very well.

Your goal as a cancer patient is to find a doctor with broad experience in dealing with your particular disease. Whether an experienced surgeon, an experienced radiation oncologist, or an experienced medical oncologist, you want someone who has treated a lot of patients with your type of cancer and can deal with the side effects and occasional setbacks that most cancer patients encounter.

You do not want to be the patient that your doctor[s] "go to school" on!

TIP #5

IF YOU HAVE A POOR PROGNOSIS AND/OR ARE TOLD YOU HAVE A "RARE" FORM OF CANCER, TRY TO GET TO A "CENTER OF EXCELLENCE" – AT LEAST FOR A *SECOND OPINION*.

My own experience demonstrated that there is sometimes a significant gap between what you are offered by your local physician and what is available "out there" somewhere.

If you are told that your cancer is "rare" or that you have a "poor prognosis," it may simply mean that your doctor lacks confidence that you can or will be cured, or it may mean that he or she has not treated many of these cancers. In these cases, you need to find a doctor or an institution that is focused on your disease and has the broadest possible experience with it. These are also the places most likely to be doing exciting research and having the best results with this disease.*

Gay, a young mother, called me at the suggestion of a friend. She was devastated to learn from her doctors that she had small-cell lung cancer, a particularly aggressive and virulent form of the disease. Only a small percentage of persons with this disease are alive a year after diagnosis.

I commiserated with this stranger over the phone and struggled to find something truthful to say that was even mildly encouraging. I promised to go on the Internet and see if there were any interesting clinical trials being conducted for small-cell lung cancer . . . but I did not expect to find anything. I was surprised to stumble onto a small vaccine trial that had been conducted at Sloan-Kettering

---

* There are cancer "centers of excellence" in every area of the country: Duke in the South, Johns Hopkins in the Mid-Atlantic, Sloan-Kettering in New York, Dana-Farber in Boston in the Northeast, M. D. Andersen (Houston) in the Southwest, Mayo Clinic in the Midwest, and so on. I recommend *U.S. News & World Report*'s "Best Hospital" annual survey written by Avery Comarow, which ranks hospitals by specialty and disease.

Cancer Institute by Dr. Stefan Grant. He had developed and tested his vaccine on seven patients with small-cell lung cancer in 1994. Three years later, five of these patients were free of disease . . . a remarkable outcome for this dangerous cancer.

I tried to restrain my own excitement when I called Gay; the last thing in the world she needed was false hope. I knew that there might not be new trials actively underway or, even worse, that she might not qualify. I faxed her the abstract on Dr. Grant's study and strongly recommended that she have her physician look into it.

Her doctor was not familiar with Grant's work and discouraged Gay from pursuing it — on the theory that Grant's trial involved a "tiny number" of patients. Gay and I enjoyed a laugh about his parochial reaction. True enough, it was a "tiny trial," but if you had small-cell lung cancer, wouldn't you have liked to have been one of the seven people in that trial?

Gay, a strong-willed woman determined to see her young children grow up, gathered her records and forged ahead. She went to Dr. Grant and was admitted into an expanded version of his vaccine trial.

That was three years ago, and today Gay is still alive. She is not free of cancer but has fought it to a standstill and has enjoyed several years with her family that she could not have counted on with the treatment offered her by her first doctors.

At the end of the day, I never expected any doctor to personally guarantee me a "cure." But I always tried to find a doctor who could look me in the eye, give me hope, and hold out at least the possibility of my being cured. If my doctor were to tell me that I was going to die, that would unleash (at least in me) a cascading series of events emotionally and physically, with my shattered belief in being cured ultimately signaling to my body that it was okay to stop fighting.

At that point, I would be as good as dead.

TIP #6
DO NOT ALLOW YOUR CAREGIVERS TO PROJECT THEIR VALUES, GOALS, AND EXPECTATIONS ONTO YOU.

I recently counseled a 68-year-old man who was diagnosed with prostate cancer — aggressive, but still confined to his prostate. A very active and otherwise healthy man, he works every day and plays a vigorous game of tennis three or four times a week.

His 35-year-old urologist told the gentleman's daughter, "Your father's life expectancy is about five or six years. If we do nothing or put him on female hormones, he will almost certainly live three or four more years before developing serious symptoms. Why put him through tough surgery or radiation just for the possibility of a few extra years?"

The man, unwilling to let a doctor half his age play "God" with his life, went ahead with the surgery, which he tolerated very well. Today, he is back at work, playing tennis, and claiming he will live to be ninety. While living to be seventy-five may have seemed a reasonable goal for a 35-year-old doctor, it was not long enough for this 68-year-old man in good physical and emotional health.

The well-intentioned young doctor thought he was being compassionate in urging "watchful waiting" and avoiding major surgery. But he was projecting *his* expectations about life onto his patient . . . who had very different expectations.

TIP #7
UNDERSTAND THE ECONOMICS OF CANCER CARE.

I believe that physicians — as a group — are the hardest-working and most well-motivated professionals in our society. But in the past decade, they also have had to face up to the harsh realities of the economics of health care.

It is difficult to overstate the financial pressure on physicians today, in every professional setting. More than they like or want to admit, doctors have to consider increasingly the financial implications of their medical advice and decisions.

A cancer patient cannot afford to be either naive about or oblivious to the economic consequences of health care today. This is just one more factor in the decisions that the cancer patient — and the doctor — have to make. Encourage your doctor to provide you his or her best advice . . . regardless of what your insurance covers. *You* decide whether or not you can afford to act on that advice.

TIP #8

Ultimately, find a doctor you trust and believe in . . . but don't expect him or her to be perfect.

Doctors are only human, and very few have the "total package" — great skills, extensive experience, up-to-date knowledge of the latest treatments, a wonderful bedside manner, plenty of time to console you and your family, etc.

Indeed, the better the doctor, the more likely that he or she will not have everything that you want and need . . . particularly a lot of time. In the last analysis, I decided that I wanted a doctor whom I could trust and one who thought he could cure me of my disease . . . regardless of the statistics.

On the other end of the spectrum, I have seen cancer patients study these decisions to death (almost literally) — which doctor to use, which treatment to undergo — sometimes as an unconscious excuse to avoid a difficult surgery or chemotherapy. Some cancers grow very quickly, and months and even weeks can be critically important. Others grow slowly. It was always my attitude never to give the cancer an extra day or minute to grow. I couldn't stand the thought of a single cell breaking off from the primary tumor, migrating to some distant site, and showing up a year or two later to cost me my life.

Move deliberately, make good decisions, and don't look back . . . save all of your physical and emotional energy to tolerate your treatment and to defeat your disease.

TIP #9

DON'T FORGET TO "TREAT" YOUR MIND AS WELL AS YOUR BODY.

Once you understand your cancer, have found the best possible doctor, and are receiving the best possible treatment[s], it will still be necessary for you to deal with the mental challenges of having cancer.

- How do I get through the difficult treatments?
- Do I share or hide my real fears and feelings from my loved ones and children?
- Even with a good prognosis, how do I live from checkup to checkup?
- What if my cancer returns?
- What are the things that I can do that will fortify my body and my mind as I fight cancer?

Some doctors are neither well trained nor very good at this part of their job. Focused on very sick patients not doing well, struggling to keep up with the rapid pace of technology and new treatments, challenged on all sides by the changing economics of health care, *many*

*physicians are not very helpful in dealing with the emo-
tional challenges of cancer.*

Most doctors have difficulty coping with that which
cannot be understood or quantified or related to the
specific illness they are treating. When I asked my first
clinician at NCI — a wonderful young doctor — what I
should do about my "head," he suggested that I main-
tain a "positive attitude" . . . but he had no clue as to
how I might go about it.

For some help with this difficult issue, see Tip #10.

TIP #10
YOUR ATTITUDE AND BELIEFS ARE YOUR MOST POWERFUL WEAPONS AGAINST CANCER.

In many ways, the most exciting, unexplored, and confusing element of modern medicine is called the mind-body
connection, referring to the impact of a patient's attitude
on the course of a disease. I know from personal experience and through the examples of thousands of cancer
patients that attitude can affect the course of cancer in a
powerful way.

However, just as we know the universe has achieved
some kind of perfect balance we do not understand, the
exact workings of the mind-body connection remain
beyond our full comprehension. Consequently, it is
important that people do not seek spiritual remedies that
either ignore or undermine their medical treatment.

THE HAPPY WARRIORS

At the National Cancer Institute — a huge, bland federal complex — where I underwent experimental chemotherapy for my non-Hodgkin's lymphoma, the medicine was great, but the emotional support was almost nonexistent. I had expected that there would be some organized group or program, but there was not.

I quickly learned that there were two groups of patients. One group kept to themselves, did not talk or socialize, and buried their long faces in a magazine or book when they came to the clinic. These people had cancer, and their resentment and bitterness about their fate was almost palpable. If you tried to engage them in conversation, they would either cut you off or ignore you.

On my first visit to get chemo, I nervously attempted to make conversation with a bald-headed young woman seated next to me, probably hoping for some words of encouragement. When I asked her what kind of cancer she had, she turned, glared, stood up, and started shouting in my face, "Mind your own business, asshole . . . you don't care about my problems and I damn sure don't care about yours!"

These poor people were alone and had deliberately cut themselves off from family and friends. They expected to die and — more often than not — they did.

The other group of patients were the "happy warriors" who had loosely organized themselves — with little help from NCI — into an effective support group.

Regardless of their disease or prognosis, these patients would bring cookies for the nurses, tell funny stories to other patients, give hugs to those having a difficult time, and sit and hold the hands of those suffering and dying from cancer. The "happy warriors" were enjoying every minute of life in spite of their cancer, were nurturing to and nurtured by others and were determined to live every day to the fullest. They were marching to the beat of a different drummer . . . possibly to Bonnie Raitt, who sings, "Life seems more precious / When there is less of it to waste."

Over time, it became clear to me that the "happy warriors" were the ones who greatly outlived their prognosis, were often cured, and sometimes even beat supposedly incurable diseases.

It did not take me long to figure out which group I wanted to belong to, and I learned that one of the best ways to "belong" was to volunteer to welcome and indoctrinate new patients. As I did this, I felt a pressure to practice what I had preached and found that the responsibility of trying to help other patients through their ordeal was good for my own emotional state. It truly was a case of feeling blessed by giving to others.

UTILIZING YOUR ASSETS

Your doctor, nurses, and medical team bring their years of training and experience to bear in trying to defeat your cancer. You can and should be an active and important partner in your treatment. The most important things you can contribute are your own beliefs and attitude.

The natural state of the human body is good health. Each day, our body's immune system recognizes and kills germs and cancer cells gone awry. Indeed, it has been proven that a person's immune system is at its strongest and most effective in preventing and fighting disease when a person is happy, positive, and engaged.

In the last ten years, scientists have begun to demonstrate through sanctioned research trials the impact of attitude and the "will to live" on the course of disease. A study of women with metastatic breast cancer conducted by Dr. David Spiegel proved to be a landmark event in the evolution of mind-body science.

Spiegel took a large group of women with advanced breast cancer who had — overall — very poor prognoses. The group was divided into two subgroups, each containing the same number of women with the same types of breast cancer in the same stages of disease. One subgroup was left to its own devices and not provided any help or emotional assistance. The other group was supported emotionally and nurtured throughout, met as a group regularly, sang songs, played games and formed bonds of friendship, love, and common purpose.

Five years after the experiment began, there were four times more women still alive in the subgroup that was emotionally supported than in the group that was not supported. Spiegel's study was widely acclaimed, but some skeptics debunked it as "fraud." Five years later, a second study yielded results almost identical to Spiegel's.

We are only beginning to understand the impact of the mind on the course of illness. But we have to recognize it as a reality of human existence. I have seen it time and again — at NCI, at Camp Sunshine, at Johns Hopkins, in my relationships with hundreds of cancer patients — the will to live and a person's belief play a powerful role in the course of cancer and in the ultimate outcome of the illness.

WHAT CAN I DO?

Beyond the initial shock of diagnosis, the question that I am often asked by cancer patients is, "What can I do about my head? How can I get used to the idea of having cancer, living with it, possibly dying from it? What can I do emotionally to live with this new reality and to augment my medical treatment?"

There is no single or simple answer. I tell cancer patients that they have to search their own conscience, their own belief system, and their own spirituality to find that which is most comfortable for them.

MIND-BODY MEDICINE: WHAT IS REAL & WHAT IS BUNK?

The first admonition in the Hippocratic Oath, which physicians are sworn to uphold, is "Do no harm" to those patients they are trying to help.

My basic advice to all cancer patients is to "do no harm" to the medical treatments that you are receiving. Don't do anything that might actively compete with, undermine, or even threaten to undermine the impact of your medical treatment.

I look at anything else patients want to do — reasonable diets, meditation, exercise, visualization, prayer, religious rites, etc. — as being tremendously important and positive, complementary, and supportive of their medical treatment *as long as it makes patients feel good about themselves and what they are doing.*

Beyond that, I can only reiterate that your attitude and your beliefs are your greatest strengths in your battle against cancer. Use them!

PROSTATE CANCER:
WHAT YOU SHOULD KNOW AND DO*

Because of the sharp increase in the incidence of prostate cancer (probably a result of improved methods of early detection and a swell of male Baby Boomers over fifty) and the many questions surrounding treatment options, I have addressed below some specific advice for all men over forty and particularly men with either broadly defined "prostate problems" and/or a history of prostate cancer in their families – defined as fathers, brothers, and uncles.

* Note: The advice offered here is a summary of the most important facts that I have learned about prostate cancer from the most knowledgeable medical sources as a result of my own prostate cancer. It also reflects my own aggressive attitude on screening *and* treatment after three bouts with cancer. However, I am not trying to play doctor here, so *CHECK THIS OUT WITH YOUR OWN FAMILY DOCTOR OR UROLOGIST!*

1. STARTING AS EARLY AS AGE FORTY AND CERTAINLY BY AGE FORTY-FIVE, EVERY MAN SHOULD HAVE AN ANNUAL PHYSICAL EXAMINATION.

This includes a DRE (digital rectal exam), in which a doctor palpates your prostate for lumps or abnormalities, as well as a PSA (blood test) specifically designed to detect prostate cancer.

The Digital Rectal Exam (or DRE)

This is the age-old test for prostate cancer which allows the physician to feel your prostate for lumps, hard areas, and irregular surfaces that *may* indicate prostate cancer. Many men shun this simple test and find it embarrassing. It only takes several seconds and – though slightly uncomfortable – could save your life.

The PSA (Prostate-Specific Antigen) Test

In the last decade, an important new diagnostic test was developed and offered to men called the PSA. The growth of prostate cancer in your body produces an antigen which can be detected by a blood test. It is not an infallible test, as many men will have an elevated PSA but will not have prostate cancer. However, for many men with prostate cancer, *the PSA is the only way to detect early growth while the cancer is still confined to the prostate gland and highly curable.*

• There are two critical factors in evaluating the PSA: the *total numerical "reading"* and the *"velocity."* The *reading* produces a numerical value, and a high number requires further investigation. The *velocity* tells you how much the PSA has increased since your last test. *A high PSA number is a reason for concern, as is an increase in the PSA of more than .75 in a year or less.*

• An *abnormal* PSA is a reading that exceeds the upper limit on the following chart, which was developed by the Mayo Clinic and is adjusted for age. While many family physicians only consider a PSA reading in excess of 4.0 to be abnormal, this age-adjusted chart is a more precise diagnostic tool.

PSA RANGES (ADJUSTED FOR AGE)

Age	Normal	Abnormal
40 – 49	0 – 2.5	over 2.5
50 – 59	0 – 3.5	over 3.5
60 – 69	0 – 4.5	over 4.5
70 – 79	0 – 6.5	over 6.5

2. IF YOUR PSA AND DRE ARE BOTH NORMAL, THE ODDS ARE OVERWHELMING (ALMOST 95 PERCENT) THAT YOU DO NOT HAVE PROSTATE CANCER.

However, these individual tests, taken alone, are much less significant and conclusive. *You need BOTH tests taken at the same time to provide a high degree of confidence that your prostate is normal.*

3. ONCE YOU HAVE HAD A NORMAL EXAMINATION YOU NEED TO HAVE REGULAR ANNUAL EXAMINATIONS.

The only way to benefit from the PSA test and the DRE is for your doctor to establish a "baseline" and to measure any changes that take place.

4. AN ABNORMAL PSA OR DRE REQUIRES ADDITIONAL INVESTIGATION.

If your physician or internist discovers an abnormal finding through the DRE or a "rising PSA," he or she will order additional tests and will probably send you to a urologist, a specialist in dealing with prostate cancer.

5. IF YOUR PSA READINGS ARE MODERATELY HIGH OR VERY HIGH, YOU SHOULD IMMEDIATELY HAVE AN ULTRASOUND AND POSSIBLY A BIOPSY.

If your PSA is "borderline high" and a possible aberration, your doctor may suggest that you have your PSA retested in a couple of months.

6. A LUMP OR IRREGULARITY IN YOUR PROSTATE REQUIRES AT LEAST AN ULTRASOUND AND A POSSIBLE NEEDLE BIOPSY OF THE SUSPICIOUS AREA(S).

7. BY INSERTING A SMALL SCOPE IN YOUR RECTUM, THE ULTRASOUND ALLOWS YOUR UROLOGIST TO "SEE" YOUR PROSTATE AND DETECT ABNORMALITIES.

This test has a high number of false-positive readings because a common infection of the prostate (prostatitis) can present itself on the ultrasound in a way that mimics prostate cancer.

8. THE NEEDLE BIOPSY IS THE ULTIMATE PROSTATE TEST BECAUSE IT ENABLES THE UROLOGIST, USING THE ULTRASOUND AS A GUIDE, TO SAMPLE TISSUE FROM SUSPICIOUS AREAS AND/OR TAKE RANDOM SAMPLES.

These samples are closely examined under a microscope by a pathologist to determine if cancerous cells are present. For most men, this procedure is uncomfortable but not extremely painful.

For many years, urologists took six biopsies to give them a broad sampling of the prostate tissue. Depending on the patient, the finding and the instincts of the urologist, some urologists today are more aggressive and are taking ten or even twelve samples.

9. IF YOUR BIOPSY INDICATES THAT YOU HAVE PROSTATE CANCER, GET A COPY OF THE BOOK *THE PROSTATE*, BY DR. PATRICK WALSH, READ IT TO UNDERSTAND YOUR DISEASE AND YOUR TREATMENT OPTIONS, AND THEN FIND THE BEST AND MOST EXPERIENCED UROLOGIST THAT YOU CAN!

Treatment options for prostate cancer are ultimately very personal, and individual decisions are widely debated and can be confusing to lay people like ourselves. Utilize your family doctor or internist as your "coach" to help you understand your options and to recommend the best and most experienced urologist(s) to make and execute your treatment decisions.

One valuable resource is the "Partin Tables," developed by Dr. Alan Partin of Johns Hopkins. This table is a valuable tool which can be used by your urologist or family doctor and yourself to assess your personal situation (PSA score, "staging," and Gleason score) in terms of which treatment options are best for you.

10. BE AWARE OF THE "PROSTATE HISTORY" OF YOUR OWN FAMILY.

If there is prostate cancer in your family (including your father, grandfathers, brothers, uncles, and first cousins), your odds of developing prostate cancer are significantly increased. You might want to have a urologist check you in addition to your family doctor. Your urologist does many DREs each day, has a more experienced pair of "hands" or "fingers," and a greater likelihood of catching a subtle change in your prostate.

IN CLOSING:
THE NEED FOR NATIONAL EDUCATION AND RESEARCH

Due to the tireless energy, efforts, and commitment of a remarkable group of women over the past decade, we have seen a dramatic increase in the national awareness of breast cancer, which, in turn, has resulted in more aggressive screening, increased funding, and a powerful grassroots movement. Cancer activists like Ellen Stovall and Fran Visco have shown us the way.

Unfortunately, we men have not been as effective in addressing prostate cancer on either a personal or national level. Men are much less likely than women to have regular physical examinations and less likely to follow up on unusual or abnormal findings.

However, in the past five years, there is finally

underway a vigorous national effort to prevent and cure prostate cancer.

Under the leadership of financier Michael Milken (himself a prostate cancer survivor) and through CAPCURE — a nonprofit organization largely funded by Milken — an intense and comprehensive effort has been undertaken to reach and educate males in this country and to increase both awareness of and funding for prostate cancer research.

This effort has been greatly enhanced by the willingness of men like Bob Dole, Joe Torre, General Norman Schwartzkoff, and Arnold Palmer to tell their own stories publicly about prostate cancer and to lend their names and voices to the cause of curing prostate cancer.

You can do your part by having regular physicals, following your physician's directions for follow-up visits, and supporting reasonable efforts to increase prostate cancer funding. The intersection of research, infomatics, and genetics holds the promise of both prevention and cure of this terrible disease.

SOURCES FOR INFORMATION
FOR CANCER PATIENTS

The good news is that there is so much information instantly available through the Internet to cancer patients, their loved ones, and their physicians.

The bad news is that it can be overwhelming for a lay person like myself to sort through all the available information and to separate that which is research-based and valid from that which is not. Medicine has its own language, but with persistence, I have learned that a patient or loved one can understand and use that language.

However, it would be my suggestion that you utilize your internist or family doctor to be your "coach." He or she has the best understanding of your overall health situation, your personality, and other intangibles that must feed into any decision you might make.

While there are many wonderful disease-specific sites, let me mention a handful of cancer websites that are solid, reliable, and valuable. Some are more patient-friendly, and others more appropriate for your physicians, but most have information that is tailored for both.

AMERICAN CANCER SOCIETY
www.cancer.org

The American Cancer Society is one of the oldest and most successful cancer organizations with a particular focus on the patient. This is a very useful and patient-friendly site with tons of valuable information.

NATIONAL CANCER INSTITUTE
www.cancernet.gov

This is the official site of the National Cancer Institute, the government agency that oversees the clinical trials and research funded through the federal government. Very useful.

AMERICAN SOCIETY OF CLINICAL ONCOLOGY
www.asco.org

This is the website of practicing oncologists – the physicians who actually manage and direct the care of cancer patients, with a special emphasis on clinical trials that are in progress.

AMERICAN ASSOCIATION FOR CANCER RESEARCH
www.aacr.org

This website, devoted to serious research, allows readers to keep abreast of the most promising developments from the labs.

ACKNOWLEDGMENTS

While writing a book — and particularly a memoir — is a deeply personal effort, it was enriched and made easier with the help of these friends who read my early drafts and provided me candid feedback, constructive criticism and suggestions:

Tom Beard; Jay Beck; Peter Beucher; Dr. Lan Bo Chen; Frank Fowler; Dr. Ellen Frauenthal; Steve Gorlin; David Guthrie; Sally Hale; Dr. Michael Johns; Barbara Kaufman; Tom Luce; Dr. Bill Mayfield; Joel McCleary; Sam Nunn; Alan Petroff; Vicki Riedel; Eden & Jerry Rafshoon; Debbie and Bill Rogers; Don Sallee ("Dr. Comma"); Chris Sallee; Linda and Steve Selig; Dr. Jonathan Simons; Dr. Tommy Tucker; Phil Walden; Suzanne Williamson & Peter Pollak; and Andy Young.

At Longstreet Press:

What started as a solid working relationship has evolved into a wonderful partnership with my publisher, Longstreet Press of Atlanta. The conventional wisdom was that there was not a market for a "cancer book."

Scott Bard, Longstreet's dynamic young publisher, refused to accept that conventional wisdom and believed in this book from the very beginning. Scott has given me all the advice, help, and active support that any author could want.

Senior Editor John Yow has been my guide and friend, helping to shape and define what our book should and should not be. John displays an uncanny knack for knowing when to step in and bail me out and when to back off and let me find my own way. His ideas and input combined with his sharp eye, his gift for language, and his easy wit have been invaluable to me.

My gratitude also to all the Longstreet Press team — Beth Dickey, Stacey Hartmann, Robyn Richardson, Burtch Hunter, Mark Owen, Megan Wilson — for their untiring efforts and publishing know-how. This is as much their book as it is mine.

To Dorothy:

In addition to being a phenomenal woman and mother, my wife is a lover of books and a first-class editor herself. From the very beginning, Dorothy struggled with me through the evolution of the idea for this book, its many drafts and revisions. To her, my gratitude, thanks and love.

Special thanks:

With appreciation, to Rafe Sagalyn, my agent, for his solid advice and steadfast efforts on my behalf.

Finally, my thanks to my friends at Modica Market, Seaside, Florida, whose early morning coffee and warm friendship kept me going last summer when I was writing my first draft.

A Note on Sources:

This book is a collection of events and memories from the past fifty years. While I have researched each topic to the extent possible, this work is largely dependent upon my own recollection of names, anecdotes, conversations, dates, and events from almost half a century. Any mistakes herein are entirely my own.

Clarence Jordan:

Unlike the rest of my journey as recounted in these pages, the section on Clarence Jordan is drawn not only from own memories, but also from history and anecdotes derived from other sources. I probably saw Clarence Jordan two dozen times in my life, so I relied heavily here on others who knew, wrote about, and followed him.

I want to recognize and acknowledge these major sources of information on Clarence:

> *Cotton Patch Evidence*, written by Dallas Lee, published in 1971 by Harper & Row, is the authoritative biography of Clarence Jordan. This is an excellent book and the ultimate record of Clarence Jordan's life and work.

> The Hargrett Collection, University of Georgia Library, is where Clarence Jordan's papers, correspondence, tapes, and film are stored. Thanks to the staff there for their help and support for our requests.

> Finally, in 1995 I produced a short documentary film on Clarence Jordan, which allowed us to interview and record some of the people still living who were family members and followers of Clarence Jordan. These tapes and transcripts are the basis for some of the anecdotes contained herein.

> Koinonia Farm is still an operating farm dedicated to following Clarence Jordan's original vision. The staff there have made tapes and other materials available to us for use in this book.

AFTERWORD TO THE PAPERBACK EDITION

The reaction to the publication of *No Such Thing as a Bad Day* has been overwhelming for me and my family.

Like most authors, I wanted my book to enjoy good reviews and strong sales and to turn a nice profit. But, most of all, I wanted to reach those who have or will have cancer and demonstrate through my own experiences the importance of "taking charge" of the medical decisions when confronted with this, or any other, life-threatening disease.

We did enjoy a few nice reviews, had good sales, and did make a nice profit. Most important, from calls and letters throughout the United States, we know that we did touch the lives of a number of people. And — as I told my children when writing this book — if we touched even a single life, it was well worth the effort.

Most of the letters and calls were from people who have or had cancer and who could identify emotionally with my own journey. We also received ten or fifteen letters from people who were inspired by our book to have annual checkups and screenings and who — like me — discovered their cancers early enough to have a good prognosis for a cure. It was gratifying to hear these stories of people "taking charge" of their lives and health.

The United States is experiencing an epidemic of cancer — and is doing very little about it. Forty percent of all living Americans will have cancer in their lifetimes, and that statistic will be fifty percent by the year 2010.

Yet, funding for basic cancer research, traditionally the responsibility of the federal government, has been largely flat for a dozen years. We spend one tenth of a penny of every ten federal tax dollars to research and understand a disease that will strike almost half of the American people.

We organized a volunteer group of scientists, physicians, and lay people to take these facts to the presidential campaigns of Governor Bush and Vice President Gore, both of whom lost sisters to cancer. Vice President Gore favored doubling the National Cancer Institute (NCI) budget, but not as rapidly as we believe is necessary.

Governor Bush took our message and responded to it quickly, making a speech in September 2000 in which he promised to more than double the NCI budget on a faster timetable than Vice President Gore. We will count on him to follow through with this commitment, and we will speak out if he does not!

On the personal front, I continue to enjoy my life each and every day with my wife and three children.

Following the model of Camp Sunshine, which my wife, Dorothy, started for children with cancer almost twenty years ago, we launched "Camp Kudzu" in the summer of 2000 for children who suffer from juvenile diabetes. My daughter, Kathleen, was in the first "class" and had a blast.

I still have my regular checkups and hold my breath until I get all the reports back that everything is "okay." This is the special curse of having had three cancers by age fifty. It is also the blessing of waking up every morning and being able to look at each day differently.